A secure remedy

A review of the role, availability and quality of secure accommodation for children in Scotland

Social Work Services Inspectorate for Scotland

1996

Purpose and responsibilities

Our purpose is to work with others to continually improve social work services so that:

- they genuinely meet people's needs; and

- the public has confidence in them.

Member of
Plain English Campaign
committed to
clearer communication

PEC

The Social Work Services Inspectorate
James Craig Walk
Edinburgh
EH1 3BA

Secretary of State

When he was Secretary of State for Scotland, Mr Ian Lang asked me to review secure accommodation. In doing so I have found it necessary to examine the role and availability of secure care as well as the quality of care and education provided.

My findings, conclusions and recommendations are set out in this report.

The priorities I identify are:

- to improve the availability of secure care places when they are needed;

- to deal earlier and more effectively with criminal behaviour;

- to improve assessment and planning for young people who need compulsory care; and

- to develop the role of residential schools for young people with disturbed behaviour who commit crimes.

ANGUS SKINNER
Chief Inspector of Social Work Services for Scotland

Preface

In 'Scotland's Children', the white paper on child care law and policy, the Government announced that there would be a review of secure accommodation. This is the report of that review

In deciding to carry out a review, the Government recognised that secure accommodation had to provide for young people who made heavy demands on security and on care, education and recreation. By reviewing secure accommodation, the Government wanted to prepare a programme of action to develop secure care of high quality to meet future needs. In this review therefore we have considered:

- what role secure accommodation should play;
- the availability of secure accommodation places when they are needed; and,
- the quality of care and education in secure accommodation.

The review has been based on:

- inspections by us and Her Majesty's Inspectors of Schools of all the secure units in Scotland;
- the views of the wide range of agencies that sent in comments, as well as those from interested members of the public, including members of children's panels;
- statistics and other information; and
- questionnaires to
    — the chairpeople of children's panels;
    — chief constables;
    — heads of secure units;
    — directors of social work;
    — reporters to children's panels; and
    — the boards of managers of independent units.

Following a brief introduction this report has three chapters. The first deals with the role and availability of secure accommodation and the second with the quality of care and education in secure units. The final chapter puts forward key points for a programme of action.

We are grateful to everyone who contributed to the review and, in particular, to the people who made comments in the inspections. We appreciate the ready co-operation and skill of the staff of Scotland's secure units.

SWS Inspector Mike Laxton led our team on the inspections and SWS Inspector Stuart Bond and SWS Inspector Tom Anderson helped him. HM Inspectors of Schools

Mrs Browning and Dr O'Hagan assessed the education in the units. SWS Inspector Jackie McRae reviewed cases of children who present particular problems. Dr Fiona Paterson from the Central Research Unit and Ms Lorna Osborne and Mr Raymond Wilson from our Inspectorate also helped with the review. Ms Harriet Dempster chaired the advisory group. Ms Mandy Durlick was the independent member of the team inspecting the units.

Contents

Introduction

Secure accommodation in Scotland

1   There are seven units in Scotland registered to provide secure accommodation for children aged 8 to 18. Between them, these units provide 89 secure care places. Three of the units provide 73 of the 89 places. The map below shows where the units are.

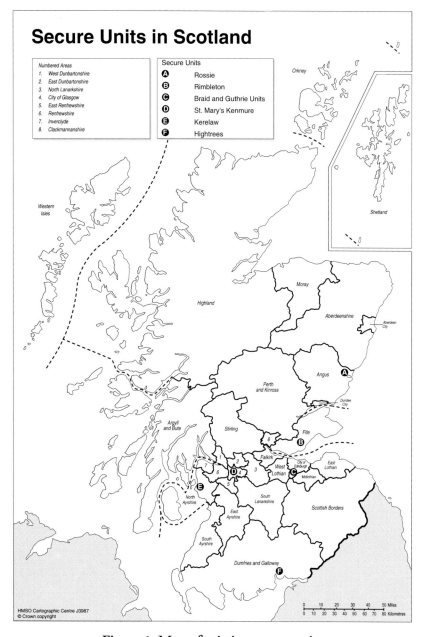

Figure 1: Map of existing secure units

1

2   The secure accommodation used for children today was mostly built in the 1960s and 1970s. People in Scotland had been concerned throughout the 1950s about some young people in care who were considered to be beyond control either because of difficult behaviour or because they often ran away. In 1962 Rossie Farm School near Montrose, which already had an established approved school providing over 100 places for boys, opened the first secure care unit for children in Britain. It provided 15 beds for boys. The first similar unit to open in England was at Kingswood in 1964. Rossie's isolated site 5 miles from Montrose and 2 miles from the main road, might have been a benefit, particularly because running away was one of the main reasons for children being taken in. Today Rossie has 25 secure places and 5 open places that prepare young people for returning to the community. There is a Board of Trustees to manage the unit. You will find a short history of the school in Annex 1.

3   In 1976, 14 years after the secure unit at Rossie opened, another unit opened at St Mary's Kenmure, an approved school in Glasgow set up by the Catholic Church in 1967. This unit had 18 beds and was originally planned for 12 boys and 6 girls. Because of demand though, it only took boys at first. The original school has now been demolished and today St Mary's Kenmure has 24 secure places, including 6 for girls, and 10 open places in a house next to the secure unit.

4   The third largest secure unit is Kerelaw School, North Ayrshire. Building started on the school in 1976 and it was finished in 1979. The school opened in 1983. Kerelaw has 24 secure care places in a unit next to an open residential school with 50 places. It is owned and managed by Strathclyde Social Work Department.

5   Between 1975 and 1988, four local authorities also opened smaller secure units in the Observation and Assessment Centres which they then had as part of their residential child care provision. Howdenhall in Lothian (Edinburgh) had five beds. The other three units (in Central, Dumfries and Galloway, and Fife) each had two beds. Today Edinburgh has two secure units next door to each other. The most recently built of these is the Guthrie unit, which opened in 1994 with seven secure places. The unit is in St Katharine's, which has two other units with eight open beds. The other unit in Edinburgh is the Braid unit in Howdenhall with five secure places. Howdenhall is a children's home with education, which also has ten open beds. Central Region closed the secure unit at the Brodie Youth Care Centre at Polmont in 1994. The two-bedded units in Fife (Rimbleton) and Dumfries and Galloway (Hightrees) are being reviewed by their local authorities.

The framework of law, regulations and guidance

6   Secure accommodation must follow the laws and rules governing all residential care for children. It must also follow statutory controls governing how secure accommodation should be run and how young people should be taken in and kept there.

7   Articles 37 and 40 of the United Nations Convention on the Rights of the Child set out a number of rules about children's freedom. You will find the relevant text from these Articles in Annex 2. The two main points of Article 37 are:

'(b)   no child shall be deprived of his or her liberty unlawfully or arbitrarily. The arrest, detention or imprisonment of a child shall be in conformity with the law and shall be used only as a measure of last resort and for the shortest appropriate period of time.'

'(c)   ...... in particular every child deprived of liberty shall be separated from adults unless it is considered in the child's best interests not to do so....'

8   When they approved the UN Convention, the UK government reserved the right not to apply rule (c) 'where at any time there is a lack of suitable accommodation or adequate facilities for a particular individual...'

9   Before the UN Convention the European Convention on Human Rights had already led to new Scottish laws. These are in the Social Work (Scotland) Act 1968 which was changed in 1983 by the Health and Social Services and Social Security Adjudications Act 1983. The 1983 Act made sure that the laws and practices relating to secure accommodation for children were in line with the European Convention on Human Rights. Since 1983, the Government has made detailed rules and guidelines for secure accommodation for children. The law sets out certain criteria that must be met before young people can be taken into secure care. It also makes sure that children do not remain in secure care any longer than necessary. Under the Secure Accommodation (Scotland) Regulations 1983, secure accommodation has to be approved by the Secretary of State. The rules and guidelines are there to make sure that the children receive suitable care and treatment and that the units are properly managed.

10   The Children (Scotland) Act 1995, mostly comes into force in April 1997. Replaces the 1968 Act and has one important change for secure accommodation. The new Act refers to the 'placing' or 'keeping' of a child in secure accommodation, rather than to the 'detaining' or 'detention' of a child. The Local Government Etc. (Scotland) Act 1994 cancels the requirement of the Social Work (Scotland) Act 1968 that local authorities must appoint directors of social work. This Act, which came into force in April 1996, means that local authorities must appoint chief social work officers and changes all the laws and rules so that instead of referring to a 'Director of Social Work' they refer to a 'Chief Social Work Officer'.

11   The law provides two main routes for taking a child into secure accommodation. If the child is waiting to go to court or has been convicted of a serious offence, they may be sent into a secure unit under the Criminal Procedure (Scotland) Act 1975. (This Act will be replaced in April 1996 by the Criminal Procedure (Scotland) Act which brings together the 1975 Act and the changes made in it.) The more common route is through the Children's

Hearings system under the Social Work (Scotland) Act 1968. There are also emergency procedures. No child can be kept in secure accommodation for more than seven days in a row or for seven days in a month, without the authority of a Children's Hearing or a Sheriff.

12   There are four categories of children who are taken into secure accommodation on court orders. These are:

- children convicted of murder and sentenced under Section 205 of the Criminal Procedure (Scotland) Act 1975;

- children convicted of other serious offences and sentenced under Section 206 of the same Act;

- children sentenced, under Section 413 of the same Act to be kept in residential care for a period of up to one year; and

- children sentenced under section 23, 24 or 297 of the 1975 Act to a local authority or to custody in a place of safety if the local authority, not the court, can choose the place of safety.

13   Children sentenced under Section 205 or 206 are assessed as soon as they arrive in secure accommodation. They are usually kept there for longer periods than other children, in some cases for several years and even until they are old enough to go to an adult prison. The Secretary of State makes all the decisions about placing children under Section 205 or 206. The local authority decides where to send children sentenced under Section 413.

14   A Children's Hearing may decide that a child on a supervision requirement under Section 44 (1) (b) of the Social Work (Scotland) Act 1968 may be put into secure care. Before deciding this the Children's Hearing must be sure that the legal criteria have been met. These criteria are set out in Section 58A of the Social Work (Scotland) Act 1968. The full text of Section 58A is provided in Annex 3. The criteria are set out in Section 58A (3). They are:

'(3) Where a children's hearing decide, in accordance with section 44 of this Act, that a child is in need of compulsory measures of care, and they are satisfied that either-

(a) he has a history of absconding, and-

(i) he is likely to abscond unless he is kept in secure accommodation; and

(ii) if he absconds, it is likely that his physical, mental or moral welfare will be at risk; or

(b) he is likely to injure himself or other persons unless he is kept in secure accommodation,

they may make it a condition of a supervision requirement under subsection (1) (b) of the said section 44 that the child shall be liable to be placed and kept in secure accommodation in the named residential establishment at such times as the person in charge of that establishment with the agreement of the director of social work of the local authority required to give effect to the supervision requirement, considers it necessary that he do so.'

When a Children's Hearing has decided on secure care, this decision only lasts for three months unless a hearing renews it because the criteria still apply.

15   Children's Hearings allow children to be kept in secure care 'at such times as the person in charge of that establishment, with the agreement of the Chief Social Work Officer required to give effect to the supervision requirement, considers it necessary'. Hearings do not make orders that a child should stay in secure care for any fixed period and they do not say that a child must go into secure accommodation. But if the members of the Hearing make it clear that they expect the child to go into secure care immediately, the local authority will arrange this if a place is available. The child will then be moved to open accommodation if secure accommodation is no longer necessary. This means that some children who have had 'secure care authorisations' made about them by Children's Hearings are not in secure accommodation. In a few cases, their behaviour may improve so much that secure accommodation never needs to be used.

16   This review of secure care, like the laws and rules, is based on the principle that no child should be in secure care for longer than necessary. This is a principle of the UN Convention on the Rights of the Child, and the European Convention on Human Rights. It is given legal power in Scotland through Sections 58A to 58E of the Social Work (Scotland) Act 1968 and through parts of the Criminal Procedure (Scotland) Act 1975. The basic principle for using secure accommodation for children is, and should always be:

> 'It should be used only as a measure of last resort and for the shortest appropriate period of time.'

> (United Nations, Convention on the Rights of the Child, 1990)

Chapter 1

The role and availability of secure care

General

Role

1 Secure accommodation can be defined as residential care with education for young people, provided in a building that the young person cannot freely leave. Secure care involves:

- controlling the young person, including taking away their freedom;

- assessing the young person's behaviour and needs; and

- providing care, education and treatment.

2 In 1985 The Scottish Office published a Code of Practice on Secure Care which describes the role of secure units. This role involves providing a high standard of child care and education that will help the young person to move back into the community. Proper care and control should be enough to keep the children securely in the unit and to make sure that they and the staff are safe. The Code emphasises that secure care should not be seen as punishment, even though it takes away the young person's freedom.

3 The role that secure care plays in Scotland's child care and justice system must be understood in the wider context of the law and other child care. Secure accommodation should only be used for children whose behaviour is a serious risk to themselves or others, and who need to have their freedom taken away until they can control that behaviour. It was designed to help small numbers of young people for short periods.

4 The behaviour which led to the child being taken into secure care is only one part of them as a whole person. It is important to remember the difference between the child and their behaviour when considering the role of secure accommodation and how best it should be managed and developed. A child may need to be in secure care from a few days to months and, in some very unusual cases, even years. But the basic role of secure care remains the same: to control, and to teach the child to control, the behaviour that made secure care necessary. Throughout this process it is important that the child should always be seen as a whole person; capable, as we all are, of good and bad.

5 Secure care is positive, active and demanding. It is not focused on punishment, and it involves much more than just holding children, waiting for them to calm down or for some other form of care to be found. Secure units hold children in a safe place and, by working directly with them and with social workers and others, change their disruptive and dangerous behaviour so that they can return to open care and education. To do their complicated work successfully, secure care units must be able to carry out in-depth assessments of the children in their care. And they must work out programmes to change

6

the children's problem behaviour. For all of this, they must have enough properly-trained staff.

Availability

6   It is important – for the child's sake and sometimes in the interests of others – that any child who needs a secure place should have one. But, equally, no child should be in secure accommodation who does not need, or no longer needs, to be there. This idea is reinforced by the cost of secure care (about £60,000 a year for each place). The aim should be to have in secure care all those who should be there, and no others; and to have all those who should be in secure care there, and nowhere else.

7   Since 1994 there have been some signs that at times there have not been enough secure places for children under 16. A few children have been sent to adult prisons because there was no secure child care place in Scotland or England. Other young people have been left in other types of care with too little support while they were waiting for a secure care place. Children's Panel members and the police have complained from time to time about a shortage of places. If places are not always available when they are needed is it because the number of secure care places is too low? Have management failures in the child care system led to increased demand for secure places? And has secure care been used as an unsuitable alternative because there are not enough open care facilities providing education?

8   Children's Hearings must be able to count on there being enough secure accommodation available when making decisions about children and young people who need this kind of care. Children should not have to go to adult prisons just because there is not enough suitable secure accommodation for them.

9   In this chapter we look at:

- the number of young people taken into secure accommodation;
- the number taken into adult prisons;
- secure care authorisations made by children's hearings;
- children placed in secure units outside Scotland; and
- young people held in police cells.

The final section contains our conclusions, which are developed in Chapter 3.

Young people taken into secure accommodation

10   The figures on young people going into secure accommodation give some idea of the demand for this kind of care. Between 1990 and 1995, the number changed each year but, as Figure 2 shows, there was no clear trend. From a total of 250 in 1990 to 91 the number of young people going into secure accommodation fell to 197 in 1992 to 93. This figure rose in 1993 to 94 to 266 and then fell again to 223 for the period April 1994 to the end of March 1995. The changes are shown in Figure 2. You will find more details in Annex 4.

Figure 2: Young people going into secure care from 1990 to 1995

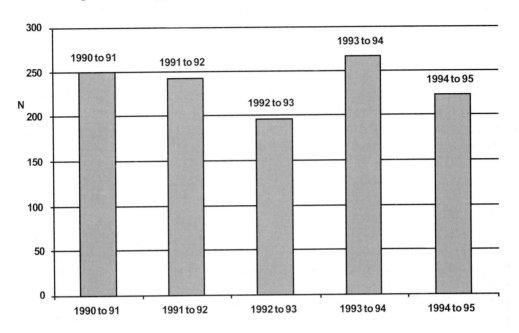

Source: Social Work Services Group Census of Residential Establishments for Children

11   There are four main points about the age and sex of the young people.

- 6 children under 12 went into secure care between 1991 and 1993. 18 went in over the following two years.

- 231 young people aged between 16 and 18 went into secure care between 1990 and 1993 (an average of 77 a year). Only 49 went in over the following two years (an average of 25 a year).

- 42% of all young people going into secure care from 1990 to 1995 were aged 15.

- More boys than girls have been taken in, although girls now make up between a quarter and a third of those taken in. The number of girls who are a danger to themselves is higher than the number of boys.

12   As we have already said, the law provides two main routes into secure accommodation: one route through court and the other through Children's Hearings. Since 1990 figures have been collected in relation to seven categories. Four of these categories relate to court cases and three to Children's Hearings.

Court route
13   There are three types of case where children can be placed in secure care after they have been sentenced. They may also be put into secure accommodation before their trial.

Section 205 cases
14   Section 205 of the Criminal Procedure (Scotland) Act 1975 says that the Secretary of State will decide where a child under 18 who has been convicted of murder should stay.

There is no time limit to this stay. If the Secretary of State sends a child to secure accommodation, the child must stay there for as long as the Secretary of State decides. These cases are very rare. From 1988 to 1995 three children have been convicted of murder (two boys and one girl).

Section 206 cases
15   Section 206 of the Act allows a court to sentence a child under 16 who has been convicted of a serious offence to be sent to a place decided by the Secretary of State. The court may decide that the child must stay there for a certain period, otherwise the child must stay for as long as the Secretary of State decides. Usually the place is secure accommodation. Between April 1990 and March 1995 there were about eight young people a year sent to secure accommodation under Section 206.

Section 413 orders
16   Under Section 413 of the Act, a Sheriff may order that a child guilty of an offence should be kept in residential care by a local authority for up to a year. In these cases, the local authority decides where the child should go. These cases are reviewed by the Director of Social Work and the officer in charge and they must apply the same criteria as apply to children placed in secure accommodation under the Social Work (Scotland) Act 1968. These are the criteria we described in the introduction (paragraph 14). Section 413 orders are now rare, with only one or two in each year since 1990.

17   The following table summarises the three types of cases where children can be placed in secure care after they have been sentenced.

	Section 205 cases	*Section 206 cases*	*Section 413 orders*
Description	The court sentences a child convicted of murder to be sent to a place which the Secretary of State decides.	A child is convicted of a serious crime and is sent to a place the Secretary of State decides. The child is always put in secure care to be assessed but may move later.	The court sentences a child to be kept in residential care by the local authority.
For how long?	No limit.	The court may fix a time, or may not.	Up to one year.
Who has the power to release the child?	Secretary of State	Secretary of State	Local authority
Use	Rare: three since 1988.	About eight each year.	Rare: one or two each year.

Place of safety
18   When a court places a child under 16 on remand before a trial, the local authority is usually responsible for keeping the child in a safe place. This may or may not be secure accommodation. However, courts do not have to hand over a child over 14 to the local authority if the child is too unruly for that to be safe. If this is the case the child will go to an adult prison. A child may also go to an adult prison if there is no secure place available.

19   The police may take a child they have arrested to secure accommodation to be kept there before the child appears in court. Or they may put the child in a police station cell if there is no other place of safety available or the child is too unruly for the place of safety offered by the local authority. When the case is heard the police must produce a certificate to prove that the child is unruly.

20   The statistics record all cases of these kinds as 'Committals to place of safety'. They are the most common reason for children going into secure accommodation under the Criminal Procedure (Scotland) Act 1975. There has been an average of 38 children going into secure accommodation as a place of safety each year since 1990. The number fell to only nine in 1991 to 92, but in 1994 to 95 it rose to 68 for no obvious reason. Demand is difficult to forecast.

All children placed in secure accommodation through the courts from 1990 to 1995
21   Figure 3 shows the changes in the number of young people going into secure units because of court decisions from 1 April 1990 to 31 March 1995. Because the numbers are fairly small the increase cannot be described as a trend. The numbers may be lower in 1995 to 1996. However, after falling from 54 in 1990 to 91 to 9 in 1991 to 92, the number of children going into secure units through this route climbed steadily to a total of 82 in 1994 to 95. The figures for 1991 to 92 may be artificially low if cases were put into different categories in the statistics then (the 'Others' category for 1991 to 1992 is unusually high). But it does seem that some courts, especially in the West of Scotland, have been sending more young people to secure accommodation in the last two to three years.

Figure 3: All children placed in secure accommodation through the courts from April 1990 to March 1994

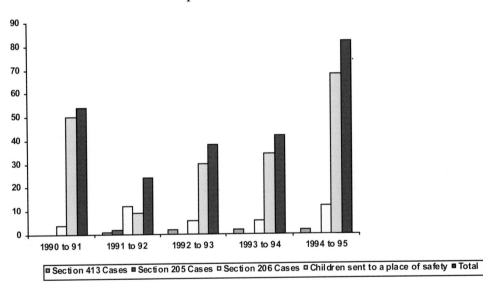

Source: SWSG Census of Residential Establishments for Children

Children's Hearings route
22   There are three types of cases where children can be placed in secure care after a Children's Hearing.

Section 44 (1) (b)

23   When a Children's Hearing decides that a child needs to go to a residential school or children's home, they make a 'supervision requirement' on the child under Section 44 (1) (b) of the Social Work (Scotland) Act 1968. The requirement should name the place the child is to go. If certain criteria are met (see paragraph 13 of the introduction), the Hearing may decide that this place could be a secure unit. The Director of Social Work and the officer in charge will decide when it is necessary for the child to be in the secure part of the unit and when in open accommodation.

24   The number of children going into secure care under Section 44 (1) (b) was quite different from year to year between 1990 and 1995. There was no clear trend. The average number was 60.

Place of safety

25   Children placed in secure accommodation provided by a local authority may be kept there if:

- they meet the criteria set out in Section 58A of the Social Work (Scotland) Act 1968;
- it is in the child's best interests; and
- the person in charge and the Director of Social Work consider it necessary.

The number of young people entering secure care in this way has averaged 50 each year from 1990 to 95.

If the Director of Social Work decides

26   In urgent cases, any children in the care of a local authority may be placed in secure accommodation. But only if the Director of Social Work and the person in charge of the unit are satisfied that:

- the child meets the criteria specified in Section 58A;
- it is in the child's best interests to be placed in secure accommodation; and
- it is necessary.

The Director of Social Work must tell the child's parents and the Reporter immediately. The Reporter must arrange a Children's Hearing within 7 days or else the child must be released. Many children go into secure accommodation in this way, but they only stay there if the Hearing decides that they should. The number of young people entering secure care in this way averaged 68 a year between 1990 and 1994, but fell to 34 in 1994 to 1995.

27   The following table summarises the three types of case where children can be placed in secure care because of a Children's Hearing.

All children placed in secure accommodation through Children's Hearings from 1990 to 1995

28   Figure 4 shows the changes in the number of young people going into secure units because of Children's Hearings from April 1990 to March 1995. The statistics show no clear trend over the period. The numbers for Section 44 (1) (b) requirements fell from 93 in 1993 to 94 to 30 in 1994 to 95 and, while this was a large fall, a similar figure was recorded

	Section 44 (1) (b) cases	*Place of Safety*	*Section 44 (6)*
Description	Secure care following a residential supervision requirement.	Children who are a risk to others or themselves.	Children in care who are a risk to others or themselves.
For how long?	No limit. Reviewed every three months.	Up to seven days. May be extended up to 70 days.	Up to seven days.
Who has the power to release the child?	Children's Hearing. Director of Social Work and officer in charge.	Children's Hearing. Director of Social Work and officer in charge.	Children's Hearing. Director of Social Work and officer in charge.
Use	About 60 each year. Covers most of the children in secure care, including many taken in under other emergency orders.	About 50 each year. Most are converted to Section 44 (1) (b) cases.	About 60 each year.

for 1992 to 93. The figures only show the children who actually went into secure care; the number who could have been taken into secure care is higher than this. It is hard to assess the figures accurately because they are fairly small.

Figure 4: All children placed in secure accommodation through Children's Hearings from 1990-91 to 1994-1995

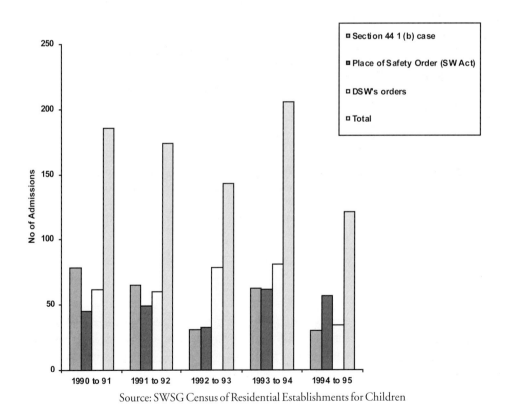

Source: SWSG Census of Residential Establishments for Children

Comparing the two routes

29   As figure 2 showed, the total number of children going into secure care has changed over the five years from 1990 to 95 without any obvious trend. The numbers entering through the two different routes also changed each year, with more children coming through the court route in 1994 to 95.

30   Figure 5 shows the numbers going into secure care through each route for each year from 1990 to 91 up to 1994 to 95. This shows how the percentage of young people that came through the court route increased in 1994 to 95 and the percentage coming through the Children's Hearing route fell. As the total number of beds has not changed and, in fact, several beds were out of use for some of 1994 to 1995, the increased number of children entering through the courts in 1994 to 95 restricted the number available to Children's Hearings.

Figure 5: Percentages of children entering secure care through the court route and the Children's Hearings route from 1990 to 1995

Source: SWSG Census of Residential Establishments for Children

31   These figures by themselves do not show that there is a shortage of secure accommodation. This is because they do not include information about children who would have been in secure care if there had been places available. To help us assess this shortage, we must look at the number of children who are in prison and the number who Children's Hearings have agreed could be taken into secure care.

13

Children under 16 who are sent to prison

32 Under Sections 24 and 297 of the Criminal Procedure (Scotland) Act 1975 a child over the age of 14 who is charged with an offence may be sent to prison if the court considers them too unruly for local authority care. Over the last ten years, fewer and fewer children have been sent to prison on 'unruly certificates'. Figure 6 shows the details.

Figure 6: Unruly certificates from 1984 to 1994

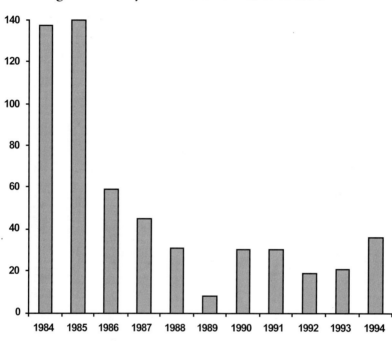

Source: Scottish Office Statistics

33 Since 1994, more children under 16 have been put in prison. Estimated figures show that Longriggend took in 63 children under 16 under unruly certificates in the eleven months up to 1 December 1995. This is still far lower than the 1984 totals, but the increase is a matter of serious concern. Almost all children under 16 with unruly certificates are sent to Longriggend Remand Centre rather than a local prison. However, going to any prison would not be in their best interests unless there was nowhere else they could be held safely.

34 Many of the children sent to adult prisons are there for only a short time (even just a day or two). Others may be there for several weeks or months. Examining the figures for April 1994 to March 1995 showed that on any one day, the number of children under 16 in prison ranged from 0 to 10. We do not know why all of the children were there, but it seems that a few of them were such a high risk to themselves and others that prison was the safest place for them. The others were probably there because there was no suitable secure accommodation available.

Secure care authorisations by Children's Hearings

35   Most children are placed in secure accommodation by a Children's Hearing under Section 44 (1) (b). This is known as a 'secure care authorisation'. As Figure 7 shows, the number of these authorisations shows a small but steady rise from 84 in 1984, when they were introduced, to 120 in 1994.

Figure 7: Secure care authorisations by Children's Hearings from 1984 to 1994

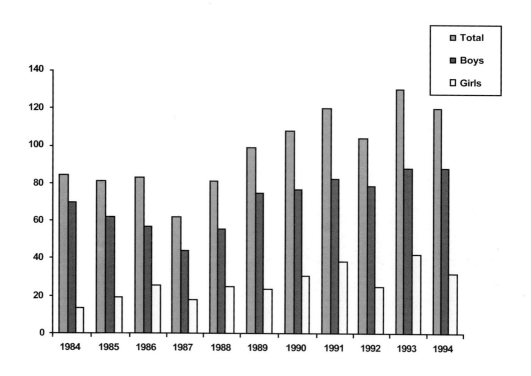

Source: SWSG Children's Hearings Returns.

36   The average number of girls with secure care authorisations in each of the years between 1984 and 1988 was 20 and for the years between 1989 and 1994 it rose to 32. However the number of boys also rose, and girls still only accounted for between a quarter and a third.

37   The most recent figures (1990 to 1993) for each region are shown in Figure 8. Over this period about 70% of all authorisations were made in Strathclyde (38%) and Lothian (31%). Smaller authorities such as Grampian, Tayside and Fife showed greater differences from year to year because of the small numbers involved.

Figure 8: Secure care authorisations by region from 1990 to 1993

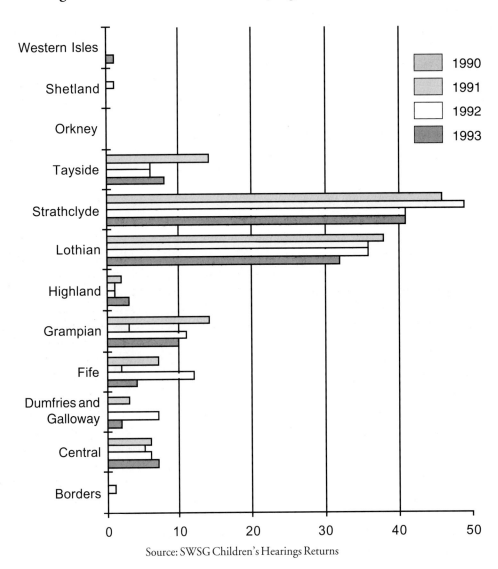

Source: SWSG Children's Hearings Returns

38   These figures show a higher number of secure care authorisations in Lothian, compared with other Regions, than might be expected for the size of its population. There are several possible reasons for this. One is that in Lothian more young people with serious offences are dealt with by the Children's Hearings rather than being dealt with by the courts. Another is that children in care in Lothian are more likely to be moved on to a secure place rather than being left in the place they are experiencing their problems. Or it may be that Lothian's figures are not high, but the other figures are low. It seems likely that there is a mixture of reasons.

39   There are differences in the procedures used following secure care authorisations. Cases referred to Kerelaw and St Mary's, Kenmure (which are mainly from the West of Scotland) are considered first by an Admissions Panel chaired by one of the two unit heads. The panel considers that its tasks are to decide:

- whether secure care is in the best interests of the child at that time; and
- which children need to go into secure care first.

The panel also provides useful advice for cases referred to it by social workers and others.

40   Many secure care authorisations in Strathclyde do not name a particular unit. This is because the Admissions Panel usually decides where to send the child. This practice should be reviewed. In 'Children's Hearings and the Sheriff Court', Sheriff Kearney argues that:

> 'The residential establishment chosen must be 'named in the requirement' and a requirement that 'the child is required to reside in a residential establishment' (no specific name being given) has been held to be invalid.'

41   We carried out a survey in 1994 and found that of 22 children with secure care authorisations, 14 were placed immediately in secure care. Of the others, 3 were put into secure care after staying somewhere else. A survey by the Association of Directors of Social Work in April 1995 found that on a certain day there were 24 children (including 6 girls) with secure care authorisations who were not in secure accommodation. Six of these children had been placed in secure care and moved on to open accommodation. Ten of the children had been placed immediately in an open school or home (with extra support), and this was considered to be meeting their needs for care and control. However, in 6 of the 24 cases there was no doubt that the child should have been in secure accommodation. The reason they were not was that there were no places available. Four of these six children were in a residential school or home, one was at home and one was in Longriggend.

42   There are no national figures of the number of children waiting for a place in secure care. It seems, however, that the position reported in April 1995 has continued much the same since. Some Children's Panel members report that they have had to deal with cases where they wanted to authorise secure care but were told by the social worker that no place was available. It is a serious problem if children who should be in secure accommodation cannot be placed there because there are not enough places. Although figures go up and down and are difficult to interpret, we estimate that in 1995 there were (at any one time) between 6 and 16 children waiting for a place in secure care or in prison because no secure accommodation was available.

Children from Scotland sent to secure care in England

43   We do not collect statistics on the number and characteristics of young people from Scotland placed in secure units in England. However, it is possible to estimate how often this happens by looking at other information, in particular that supplied by directors of social work. Although the figures are not complete it seems that between 10 and 20 young people are placed in secure units in England each year. This is between 5% and 10% of all the young people going into secure care in Scotland in a year.

44   The reasons for this depend on each case. In most cases, the unit in England is chosen because it provides a longer-term placement or a programme that meets special needs. In a very few cases, it is because no place is available in Scotland.

Young people in police cells

45   We also need to consider the young people held in police cells. Senior police officers have the power under Section 296 of the Criminal Procedure (Scotland) Act 1975 to issue 'unruly certificates' when the police make an arrest. If they do this, they can keep the young person in a police cell for up to 7 days.

46   Section 296 (2) of the Criminal Procedure (Scotland) Act 1975 says that

'Where a child has been apprehended by the police and is not liberated under section 296 (1), the officer of police shall cause him to be detained in a place of safety other than a police station until he can be brought before a Sheriff sitting summarily unless the officer certifies:

- that it is impracticable to do so; or

- that he is so unruly a character that he cannot safely be so detained; or

- that by reason of his state of health or his mental or bodily condition it is inadvisable so to detain him.'

47   As part of its contribution to this review Strathclyde Police Force carried out a survey of all the unruly certificates they had given out in 1992 to 93. They found that there had been over 300 in Strathclyde. If we assume a 60:40 split in workload between Strathclyde and the rest of the country, this could mean that police over the whole of Scotland made 500 unruly certificates in 1992 to 93.

48   The Social Work Department is responsible for providing a place of safety. All but one police force said that if the Social Work Department offered an alternative to police cells, the police would usually accept. However, this is not consistent with the police having given out 500 unruly certificates. The Association of Chief Police Officers in Scotland (ACPOS) stated that:

'The principal link between the police and secure accommodation arises from circumstances where a young person's behaviour is such that they are certified "unruly" by the police and subsequently transferred to the care of the Social Work Department for placement in secure accommodation in order that the subsequent appearance at court or at a Children's Hearing can be reasonably guaranteed.'

49   Social work departments made the following suggestions.

- The police should ask for a place of safety in all cases where they are considering an unruly certificate.

- Senior management in the police and social work departments should improve their arrangements for communication and co-ordination.

- The arrangements for monitoring must be improved.

- Police orders and social work policy and practice guidance should be made more consistent with each other.

50   ACPOS drew particular attention to the different criteria which social work departments use when considering how suitable a child is for secure accommodation and those used by the police when considering the need for an unruly certificate. ACPOS argued that it would be better if the codes of practice of the two professions could be brought into line.

51   There are differences between what the police expect when they ask for a place of safety (a place in secure accommodation) and what social work departments offer. It also appears that many of the children given unruly certificates are already in care. If the care and control provided in children's homes and schools were strengthened, then some of the current problems would not come about. The best way to make sure of good practice and communication in these matters would be for social work departments and police forces to examine the issues together at an annual meeting in each police force area.

Recommendation 1

Each year, police and social work departments should review the arrangements and practice in each force area for children who need to be held in a place of safety before appearing in court. They should make sure that policies and practice are well co-ordinated and plan and review any improvements which are needed.

The range of views

52   The figures and other information available show that there are peak times when there is not enough secure care to meet demand. This is confirmed by the views of most of the agencies involved. The Association of Chief Police Officers (ACPOS) would like to see more local secure accommodation and enough emergency beds in secure accommodation throughout Scotland 'so that unnecessary distress to children subject to secure orders can be avoided because a place is not immediately available'.

53   Some Children's Panel members have also shown their concern that there are not enough places available. They consider that some young people are not placed in secure accommodation when they could benefit from this kind of care. Generally, regional chairs of Children's Panels believe that social work reports do consider the need for secure care if this could be suitable, but one chairperson claimed that this was not always so.

54   Regional Reporters to Children's Panels and directors of social work are worried by the shortage of suitable alternative residential care. As one regional Reporter noted, 'There is very little provision in between a children's home and Secure Care. What is required is a mixed economy of places'. Some directors reported delays in finding long-term placements for young people who were ready to move out of secure accommodation. This again blocked secure care beds which could have been made available for other children.

55   Most agencies agree that there are sometimes problems in finding secure care places when they are needed. There are peaks and troughs in demand. However, there is less agreement about how these problems have come about, how serious they are, and the best ways to solve them. Most young people taken into secure care are already in the care of a local authority. We should consider more closely the backgrounds of young people who have come into secure care and the difficulties associated with assessing and treating their

problem behaviour. Solutions to the problem need to take account of the success of other forms of care. We may not solve the real problems by just making more secure places available.

Children in secure care

56   Inspectors reviewed information held in secure units of 74 young people in secure care on a date in 1994. All but three of the young people had been in local authority care before they moved into secure accommodation. The average length of time they had spent in care was over three years (166 weeks) and the actual length of time in care ranged from a month to more than 15 years. On average, the young people in secure accommodation had been in more than four other care home or family placements, and the individual number of placements varied quite widely from 1 to 17. In these children's case records, 'breakdown of previous placement' was three times more likely to be given as the main reason for moving the young person than 'progress'.

57   The Inspectors found that most of the families of the young people had been known to the social work department for some time. For example, 81% (60) had been known to the department before the young person was taken into care. But secure unit records did not have many details about young people's family backgrounds or their history in care. This must limit their ability, and the social workers' ability, to fully assess and work with the young people.

58   Just slightly over half of the young people (58%) were considered to be a risk to others and over 83% (62 of the 74 cases) were considered to be a risk to themselves. These figures hide great differences between boys and girls. 39 of the 58 boys (67%) were considered a risk to others while this applied to only 4 of the 16 girls (25%). All but one of the girls were seen as a risk to themselves. 47 of the 58 boys (81%) were also considered a risk to themselves. Three-quarters of the young people (74%) had a history of running away. The most commonly identified problems for both boys and girls were running away (73%) and relationships with family (71%). Regular offending was the next most common problem for boys, while for girls it was substance abuse.

59   Two particularly important facts came out of this information on children in secure care. First, almost all the children have been in local authority care for a long time. Secondly, most of the young people are a risk to themselves and they all have complex behavioural problems as well as their offending behaviour.

60   The fact that so many of the young people are a risk to themselves and have complex emotional and behavioural problems emphasises the importance of good-quality assessment. Inspectors were concerned to find a cycle of incomplete assessment in several cases. This was either because of missing information or because proper follow-up work had not been done to deal with the needs and problems which had led to the child being taken into secure care.

Children who present particular problems

61   Adolescence is a time of change. Relationships are often intense and turbulent as the young person struggles to be more independent and may deliberately provoke others. Earlier methods of coping with distress or difficulties begin to fail for the young person, their parents or both.

62   Young people referred to social work departments have particular difficulties. Their needs and circumstances must be assessed carefully. A small number of them will behave disruptively and destructively causing great worry in their communities. For this small group of young people the usual residential child care provided by local authorities is often not able to provide enough care and control. In many cases the child's disruptive behaviour will have been recognised by teachers and social workers at earlier stages, sometimes from a very early age. Often, however, no effective action has been taken, or action has been taken too late.

63   We reviewed reports and information provided by social work departments about children who had died in care since 1989. We examined information about young people aged 11 or over whose deaths were not from natural causes. The causes of death included drug overdoses, solvent- and drug-related deaths, road traffic accidents where the child had taken a risk (for example by being a passenger in a stolen car), hangings and murder. We chose these cases because the children's behaviour (shown in the way they died) may have met the criteria for being taken into secure care. (They were a risk to themselves or others, and had a history of running away.)

64   Of these cases, five had caused particular problems for their families, the professionals involved and the care system. We examined these cases in more detail. There are striking similarities in the case histories of these five. All were involved in regular and serious crimes, including violent crimes. (In one case this took the form of arson and indecent assault.) All had problems early in life and had fought with their parents, seen their parents separate, or had parents involved in criminal activity. It appeared that most if not all the young people had been the victim of physical and emotional abuse or sexual abuse at home. Some had been abusing alcohol for many years without anyone helping them with this problem. And all the boys used drugs or solvents and alcohol.

65   Many young people referred to social work departments have histories of family and behaviour problems and abuse. What is most worrying about this group is that, although they often did not come to the attention of the social work department until adolescence, each showed signs of emotional and behavioural problems at a very early age. They behaved aggressively at nursery or primary schools, injured themselves and were beyond the control of their parents. All of these young people had been excluded, expelled or transferred at school but none had ever had a formal assessment of their behaviour and needs. Most were out of full-time education from early adolescence.

66   It was not always clear in how much detail the young people's deep-rooted problems were examined when the cases were assessed by the social work departments or when they went into care. The problem was made worse in each case by the fact that parents were not

willing to face up to their child's problems. This is to be expected when working with parents who have personal and practical problems of their own to deal with. Even so it is worrying that there was little evidence of parents being assessed to see how they had tried, or failed, to meet their child's needs. Finding out what had worked and what had not could, in turn, have helped to find the best way of supporting the child.

67   By considering these five cases and those reviewed in secure care we have found several common factors. In many cases:

- the child's problems have been going on for many years;

- families have asked for help but the help has not been effective or suitable;

- there is a history of care and a series of family and residential placements;

- the child has not been to school regularly; and

- residential school placements have not been considered, or have been considered too late.

68   The cases also show how important it is to:

- try to help the child and family at an early stage with their problems;

- assess the child's needs at all stages;

- deal sooner, more directly and more effectively with criminal behaviour; and

- strengthen other forms of care and education.

Conclusions

69   There are situations where a young person should be in secure care but none is available. Local authorities and others report that on several days between April 1995 and March 1996 they have not been able to find secure accommodation anywhere in the UK. Children's Panel members and the police both say that they would like to make more use of secure placements if more could be found. It appears that the courts are sending more young people under 16 to secure places and adult prisons. If a child goes to prison, this is generally because there are no secure places for children available, though there may be some cases where the court decides that the secure accommodation available is not secure enough for the child in question.

70   The court's main concern is to find a place which will hold a child safely until they return to court. If the child is sent to secure care after being sentenced, the Secretary of State must be sure that the secure accommodation they go to:

- is secure enough, with enough well-trained staff to protect the public, the child and the staff;

- provides care and treatment programmes which can deal with the child's behavioural problems and reduce the risk he or she presents on returning to the community; and

- meets the child's needs for care, education and recreation.

71   The priorities of Children's Hearings are similar to those of the court. But, because the Hearings are responsible for reviewing cases, they also look more generally at the care and control needs of the young person over a longer period. Many young people in care move far too often, from a home to a foster family or another home or school. And often these moves all happen in a short time. Hearings face particular difficulties in deciding how to deal with young people who commit offences while they are on leave from residential care, for example, committing crimes at weekends or during holidays.

72   The police's main concerns are security and restricting criminal behaviour. Secure accommodation offers solutions to the problems the police face in dealing with children who have run away from residential care or who regularly commit crimes in spite of supervision requirements, community-based projects, children's homes or residential schools.

73   We must meet the needs of all these groups. In doing so, we must also follow two legal principles from the European and UN Conventions. The first is that 'every child deprived of liberty shall be separated from adults unless it is considered in the child's best interest not to do so', and the second is that secure accommodation should only be used 'as a measure of last resort and for the shortest appropriate period of time'. At the moment these two principles are not being met. We may not always be able to meet the first, but we should always meet the second.

74   In relation to the first principle, it is worrying that the number of children being kept in adult prisons is increasing. To reduce the number, eventually to none, we will need to:

- increase the number of secure places available;

- help children's secure care units to control and treat particularly challenging and difficult young people; and

- increase the courts' confidence in other places of safety offered by local authorities, such as residential homes and schools.

75   The position of the second principle (that secure care should only be used as a last resort and for the shortest possible time) is not clear. There are times when secure accommodation is used because there is no alternative. At other times, secure care is used because other systems have failed to assess and deal with a child's difficult behaviour. Scotland's Children's Hearings System has many benefits, but it is sometimes damaged by its image among some commentators as a purely welfare-based system concerned only with children's 'needs' and not with their 'deeds'. The Children's Hearing system is, and must be, concerned with both justice and welfare, with children's deeds as well as their needs. Local authorities, who must follow through the Hearings' decisions, must therefore also look at and deal with children's deeds, including offences and disruptive behaviour, from an early age. At present the systems and services often fail to do this.

76   The fact that children in secure care have such complicated care histories emphasises the importance of strengthening other forms of care. This means looking at residential schools, and also at those children's homes, foster parents and community carers which can

take care of young people with behavioural and emotional problems and a history of crime. Our review of residential care published in 1992 highlighted weaknesses in the quality of care and education in residential care generally. Some improvements have been made but there is room for far greater progress.

77 The research reviews we carried out as part of that report showed that there is little difference between children in secure accommodation and some children in other forms of care. However, the report also showed that other forms of residential care and education have become less available over the last twenty years. In Scotland the ratio of secure beds to open beds in residential schools changed a great deal between 1981 and 1984. In 1981 there were 25 secure beds and 1,300 residential school places, a ratio of 1:68. By 1994 there were 83 secure beds and 700 open places, a ratio of around 1:9. Since 1983 the ratio of secure care authorisations to residential supervision requirements has risen and is now about 1:10. These figures suggest that, far from being used as a last resort, secure care is being used to make up for there being fewer residential school places.

78 During the 1970s and 1980s, the total number of young people fell and the numbers of young people in care, particularly in residential care, fell even more. This meant that fewer resources were needed to meet the needs of young people who committed offences or were a danger to themselves. Policy changes, such as the ending of the 'List D' category for certain schools, were not followed by policies which dealt fully with the problem of young people who committed crimes and whose behaviour was particularly difficult for others and themselves. The options have too often been limited to children's homes able to take care of young people who do not present severe problems, and secure accommodation. There are not enough resources between these two extremes, especially resources that combine care and education. Instead of dealing with young people's behaviour successfully at an early stage, our systems allow the problems to develop until they are out of the reach of ordinary resources and we can only take control by taking away children's freedom.

79 It is worrying that the demand for secure care is growing. This demand will not necessarily be met by increasing the number of secure care places. We must understand the reasons for the demand and deal with it properly. We can do this by:

- strengthening other forms of care and education;
- getting involved earlier and acting more effectively; and
- providing realistic alternatives.

80 Problems and shortages in other areas of child care contribute to increasing pressure on secure accommodation. We have quite a way to go in improving the way we manage our care and education facilities and matching them to the needs of children before we can definitely say that we need more secure places. All the groups involved might agree with this. Presumably, the police would prefer that homes and schools could prevent children running away and committing crimes, than that more and more secure places were used. Children's Hearings would surely prefer a reliable placement offering suitable care and education throughout the year rather than being faced with a choice between an unsuitable placement or secure care. And courts would presumably prefer to have suitable resources in which they had confidence rather than use an adult prison.

81   Good assessment is one of the keys to making sure that children's problems are tackled early and successfully, and that a suitable place is found for them before it is too late. The assessment must include a full social history, achievements and difficulties at school, an analysis of behaviour and a realistic outlook for the future. Too often these assessments are made too late, or not at all. Children must not be labelled as this leads them to accept their weaknesses and leads adults to underestimate the child's strengths and ability to change. However, if children's emotional and behavioural problems are to be solved then they must be dealt with at an early stage.

82   Social workers have had fewer options open to them in working with young people and in making recommendations to Children's Hearings. This is partly because of changes in policy and partly because of other pressures. Some recent developments should bring improvements. Two were announced in the White Paper 'Scotland's Children'. One is the Young Offenders Project in Central Region (funded by The Scottish Office) which is especially encouraging because the police, social workers, educational workers and a voluntary organisation are all involved. The other is the work towards setting national standards for supervising young people in the community.

83   These projects will bring benefits in the future. But they should not take our attention from the general shortage of successful community-based projects working with young people who commit offences. If secure accommodation is truly to be a last resort, there must first be other options.

84   If secure accommodation is to be used as a last resort in practice, then it must also be seen as a last resort in policy. A realistic policy should encourage suitable alternative care. We need to increase the availability of secure care. But we can do this without increasing the number of secure units. We need to manage child care resources better. We need to get involved earlier and more effectively with children who have particular behavioural problems. And we need to make sure that all the agencies involved, especially social workers and schools, work closely together so that the child is assessed properly and found a place in the right kind of care. As a result, secure care accommodation would only be used for children who needed it and beds would not be blocked with children who did not need to be there.

85   In concluding, it is helpful to compare the number of secure accommodation places in Scotland and England. Scotland has 89 secure care places for children. England has 300 secure places for children and another 200 15-year-olds in prison. Local authorities in England are to build another 170 secure places to replace the 200 places provided through the Prison Service. The Home Office plans another 200 secure training-centre places for 12-to 14-year-olds. Once all these new places are available, England will have 670 secure care places. As Scotland has roughly one-tenth of the population of England, it needs 67 places to match the total planned for the future in England. Based on this ratio, Scotland already has 30% more secure places than England plans to have, and is well provided for.

86   We conclude that the priorities are:

 • to increase the availability of secure care places when they are needed;

25

- to deal earlier and more effectively with criminal behaviour;

- to improve assessment and planning for young people who need compulsory care; and

- to develop the role of residential schools for young people with disturbed behaviour who commit crimes.

In the final chapter we discuss the action needed to deal with these points. In the next chapter we discuss the quality of care and education in secure units.

Chapter 2

The quality of care and education

This chapter sets out the main findings of our inspections and the extra information collected for the review. We have taken information from several sources to identify the needs and problems of young people, the resources available and how these resources are used. We judge the quality of care and education by setting this information in the framework of the eight principles on which residential child care should be based. These principles are identified in our report 'Another Kind of Home' published in 1992. We have printed each principle in italics at the start of the relevant section.

Individuality and development

'Young people in residential care have a right to be treated as individuals who have their own unique relationships, experiences, strengths, needs and futures, irrespective of the needs of other residents. They should be prepared for adulthood and supported until they are fully independent.'

1 This principle is particularly important for young people in secure care. Most young people in secure care have been in care for many years and have been well known to several agencies – such as social work departments, Children's Hearings, education authorities and the police. It can be difficult for agencies to continue to focus on each child's needs and problems. They tend to concentrate on controlling problem behaviour rather than dealing with its causes. When children enter secure care, the problems they have can hide their strengths and abilities.

2 All young people in secure care are given a key worker. Key workers play an important role in making sure that each young person's care and treatment are based on the needs of that young person. Key workers are usually responsible for supervising the young person's care in secure accommodation and making sure that proper links are kept with parents and important agencies and services. Teachers too have an important role in identifying and meeting educational needs.

3 In the three larger units team managers are responsible for assessing each young person and making plans and programmes for their care. However, their other responsibilities (for example, co-ordinating the day's events in the whole unit) tend to come first. This is a management problem which must be solved urgently.

Assessment
4 A secure placement can offer real opportunities for change at a vital point in a child's life. But the needs and problems of each young person must be fully assessed. The assessment should include:

- a complete social history of their family;

- the child's educational and health care needs;

- details of all the child's offences and how these have been dealt with;

- details of all incidents which have caused concern that the child's behaviour is a risk to others or themselves; and

- a description of the child's abilities and strengths which can be built on.

The child's sense of identity and self-worth should be a priority point for the assessment.

5   The quality of assessment varies and is generally far below what should be considered standard. This, together with the lengthy period over which assessments can be spread, means that many assessments are never complete. In examining case files, we found that the plans for the child were usually clear about general care needs and how to meet them. But they were less clear about how to deal with the behaviour and difficulties which led to the child being placed in secure care. The care plans also need to be reviewed regularly and carefully to measure the child's progress and identify work to be done in the future.

6   Most young people in secure care have been taken there at short notice. And the length of their stay is not fixed. However most of them, and their families, are already known to the local authority. With modern communications those arranging for the child to go into secure care should always be able to provide in advance all relevant information they have about the child. This will help the unit to prepare so that the child quickly feels that matters are under control. This does not always happen. Sometimes full information is not supplied for several days, so staff at the unit cannot arrange a suitable programme for the child.

7   Staff in secure units (including education staff) are skilled at building a direct relationship with each child. They concentrate on this as the most effective way of getting to know the child and managing the child's behaviour. Staff also need to be able to rely on having all the relevant information about, and an accurate assessment of, the child. The secure units have developed different ways of assessing children and gathering information about them. We recommend that they should agree on the best parts of their methods and consult local authorities to produce a standard admission form providing all the relevant information. Local authorities should set a standard to provide as much information as possible before the young person arrives in secure care. And they should always provide complete information within two working days so that a full assessment can be carried out. This will produce more reliable assessments and will help the staff to decide on the most suitable programme for the young person.

Recommendation 2

Secure units should review their arrangements for co-ordinating assessments of young people.

Recommendation 3

The main secure units should, after consulting local authorities, develop and agree on standard admission forms and assessment procedures.

Recommendation 4

Local authorities should give units as much information as possible on each child before the child arrives in secure care. The authorities should complete this information within two working days.

Programmes

8   The assessment should lead to a programme of care, education and treatment to meet the child's general needs. Many of these needs will not be directly related to the reasons for the child going into secure care, but the programme should provide a good quality of care and education to make up for likely gaps in the past. The programme should aim to change the behaviour which led to the child being taken into secure care. This may be so that he or she can go back to other forms of care and education or to aftercare in the community.

9   This is the practice in all units. However the programmes need extensive development. This could be achieved if:

- all units had the chance to learn from each other;
- there was more training for staff;
- the care and education programmes were better co-ordinated;
- managers paid more attention to the programme for each child and how well it was being carried out; and
- all staff knew what the aims were for each child and how they could help.

Recommendation 5

Each child in secure accommodation should have their own programme of care, education and treatment which meets their needs and aims to change the behaviour which led to them being in secure care. The programme should be decided at the end of the assessment and every member of staff should be told the aims and how they can help.

Aftercare

10   Planning for the young person's care should not only include their time in secure accommodation, but also their future after they leave. This longer-term planning is often neglected. The young person and their parents should know what is to happen at the end of secure care and that the next steps have been carefully considered. The aftercare programme should relate directly to the needs and problems of the young person.

11   Inspectors found that communication between unit staff and fieldworkers was not good. This was because some fieldworkers were inexperienced in this area or because arrangements for supervising the young person after they left secure care were not clear. Sometimes young people did not get the support they needed because resources in the community, for example accommodation, were limited.

12   For the small number of young people under Section 206 orders, aftercare should be provided in line with the National Standards for Social Work Services in the Criminal Justice System. These standards say that:

'Supervision on release is a vital element in the child's rehabilitation. Social workers responsible for the supervision of children released from detention under section 206 should seek to ensure that the supervision is informed by the principles and practice set out in the Throughcare section of the document National Objectives and Standards for Social Work Services in the Criminal Justice System, whilst continuing to take proper account of the particular personal and social needs of the child or young person.'

13   There are no national standards for aftercare for most children in secure accommodation. These children often leave secure care and find themselves in vulnerable situations. They often return to situations that had a great deal to do with their going to secure care in the first place. Many may be facing new problems such as homelessness, no job opportunities or no family or friends. It is very difficult to make an effective aftercare plan in these circumstances, and there is often a shortage of suitable resources in the local community.

Recommendation 6
Local authorities should consult secure units to agree standards for arranging aftercare and education for the children leaving secure care.

Rights and responsibilities
'Young people, children and their parents should be given a clear statement of their rights and responsibilities. They should have a confidential means of making complaints. They should be involved in decisions affecting them and in the running of the home. Their rights should be consistently respected.'

14   All secure units have clear policies on young people's rights and responsibilities, complaints procedures and the rights of parents. These policies are set out in brochures and leaflets and are given to young people and their parents at the start of secure care. The key worker should go through the rights and responsibilities with each young person during the first few days of secure care and with parents on their first visit.

15   Our Inspectors found that in general young people and their parents were aware of their rights and of the complaints procedures. Formal complaints are rare, possibly because the key worker or unit leader can deal with the problems before they get to that stage. Most young people and parents said that they were told about important decisions and were invited to review and planning meetings where they could say what they wanted.

16   Young people's meetings with staff have developed over recent years. At these meetings, they consider everyday problems in running the unit. These meetings are particularly important in the three larger units where the young people generally stay for longer periods. The meetings were organised differently in each unit, but they were all too informal and failed to check that decisions at meetings had been followed through. To get the most out of these meetings, staff must identify and follow up decisions.

Good basic care

'Young people and children in residential care with or without education, should be given a high standard of personal care. They should be offered new, varied and positive experiences of life and should be included in the wider community.'

Personal care

17   Young people in secure care or who had been in secure care in the last three years almost all spoke of the positive way they are or had been treated. For some it had been the best experience they had had in residential care. This has been found in other studies as well.

18   In general good standards of personal care are high. But it is difficult to provide varied and positive experiences of life in the restricted environment of secure accommodation. Involving young people fully in the community is not an option while they are in secure care. However, they are offered the chance to work towards outings and home leave. There is a reasonable range of leisure, sport and exercise activities for all young people in the three larger units. But attention should be given to providing leisure activities, particularly for girls.

19   Bedrooms are the only reasonably private places which young people have in secure care. But there are observation windows in the doors and staff make regular checks. Young people are encouraged to put their own posters on the walls and to bring some of their belongings for their room. However, these things cannot make up for the limitations of most of the rooms, especially in Kerelaw and St Mary's, Kenmure, which look and feel like prison cells. In Rossie and most of the local units, the bedrooms are more comfortable and private. Few rooms have cupboards or other storage space for clothes, so these have to be kept somewhere else, for example in lockers in the hall.

20   In all units, meals are normally prepared by a cook in a central kitchen and delivered to the house units. Young people were happier with the food when they had been consulted about the menu for the coming week. Units could and should offer more choice of cooked meals. Young people have access to basic foods and drinks in their house units and can prepare simple snacks.

The buildings

21   The Inspectors found serious problems with the buildings of the three major units. The smaller units had few problems. The new seven-bed Guthrie Unit in Edinburgh is good quality and sets new standards.

22   The Inspectors were particularly worried about Kerelaw and St Mary's, Kenmure. These two units are of similar design from a 1970s brief, based on prison designs.

23   In Kerelaw and St Mary's, Kenmure they have tried to adapt the buildings and improve security. However, the basic design and quality of the buildings are so poor that it is hard to see how major improvements can be made without completely rebuilding the units.

Guthrie Unit

Kerelaw

St Mary's, Kenmure

24 The main difficulties are listed below.

- There is a danger of overloading the electricity and sewerage systems.

- Ventilation is poor and causes serious problems with condensation.

- There is a shortage of space in the daily living and activity areas.

- There is a shortage of space for lessons and studying.

- There is a shortage of office space and rooms for visitors.

- Because of the two-storey design, the bedrooms are on a separate floor from the other facilities. This raises security problems. It also restricts where the young people can go and makes it more difficult for staff to do their job.

- There are no proper separate living facilities for girls.

- Piping is exposed on the inside of the building. This could be dangerous for the young people and if it was damaged it could threaten the whole unit.

- Concrete walls make it impossible to put the wires in the walls.

25 Rossie School has a generally better design and the accommodation is of a reasonable quality. However the education facility is severely cramped, which makes it very hard to provide for the very varied educational needs of the young people.

Rossie

26   The priorities for spending on buildings and equipment are set out at the beginning of chapter 3.

Education

'Young people and children should be actively encouraged in all aspects of their education, vocational training or employment and offered career guidance. Their individual educational needs should be identified and met.'

Assessing and meeting needs

27   Our Inspectors were impressed by the positive effect that education has had on many of the children and young people in secure units. Effective teaching can turn around negative attitudes to teachers and education. We found it striking that a distinction is made between the personal and professional contributions of teaching staff. Most of the pupils we interviewed appreciated the concern and commitment which their teachers showed them. They also paid tribute to members of staff who set high standards of professional practice and convinced them, as pupils, of the value and possibilities of education to change their lives and open up new horizons. Good quality education should be an important part of secure accommodation if secure care is to be successful.

28   Our Inspectors identified a number of weaknesses which affected the quality of education in secure care. Three of these are particularly important:

-   not being clear about the aims and place of education in secure units;

-   no solid policies to base education on; and

-   poor management.

29   Pupils in secure accommodation have a very wide range of educational needs. Some have great learning difficulties caused by intellectual disabilities and social, emotional and behavioural problems. Some are very able but have big problems adjusting to the demands of school and society. Many, but not all of the pupils, have had a disrupted education from, in some cases, the early stages of primary school. Some are from families where education was not seen as important. Some have become alienated from schools and resistant to any form of education.

30   To provide a complete assessment of the young person and meet their educational needs, it is important to consider the results of any educational assessments carried out on them in the past. Our Inspectors were disappointed that in over half of the cases in their survey, the unit did not know whether a young person's educational needs had been identified before they came into secure care. If the young person's needs had been identified earlier, the most common comments were 'attendance problems', 'assistance with learning difficulties' and 'attitudinal problems to education'. Arrangements for telling staff in secure units if a pupil had a formal record of needs were either not working or did not exist and Inspectors thought that the units should consider new procedures for opening and reviewing records of needs. Learning difficulties were often mentioned in the young person's current educational profile, but attendance problems were identified much less

frequently. Although young people with a history of attendance problems automatically go to school while they are in secure accommodation, skipping school may be a problem once again when they return to day school. So plans and programmes must be developed to deal with this.

31   The Inspectors believed young people would benefit greatly if a project were set up with staff in secure units to develop consistent approaches to assessing educational needs and recording progress. This project should also provide guidance on how to introduce procedures to make sure that educational records are transferred with young people to their next school. Educational needs should be assessed as part of the main care assessment.

The curriculum
32   The evidence gathered from interviews with pupils and staff and from watching what went on in the units reinforced our Inspectors' views that the curriculum in secure units should be broad, balanced and consistent, and should help pupils make progress. The Inspectors were impressed that there were groups of pupils in each unit who could analyse in detail the quality of the curriculum offered to them. Whenever possible, educational programmes should be close to the recommendations for the curriculum 5-14, to the Scottish Consultative Council on the Curriculum (SCCC) guidelines, or to the Higher Development Programme, including National Certificate courses. However, curriculum structures should not become straitjackets. They should take account of the needs of each pupil and the resources available. Some development work currently planned should offer guidance on successful curriculum structures. Pupils who are older and have lost faith in school education should be encouraged to consider the advantages of further education and vocational training.

33   Opportunities for education depend on where the secure unit is. If the unit is near a town or city, pupils can sometimes use the facilities offered by local schools, further education colleges and the community. It is easier for their teachers to get information, advice and support from colleagues in schools and from educational resource services and centres.

34   The most successful approaches to education were seen in units where educational programmes for each young person overlapped with those for groups. Pupils benefited from learning in groups as well as their own tutorials. There has been some imaginative work to involve pupils in assessing their own needs and progress. With the help of their key worker, these pupils have agreed educational targets. In terms of the curricular structures of 5-14, Standard grade courses and the Higher Skill Programme, it should be possible for teachers to plan with pupils to reach certain targets in the curriculum. To help them plan educational programmes for pupils who are in care for a short period, teachers have use of the increasing number of curriculum packages and modules which are available.

35   Our Inspectors were concerned that learning support had not been well developed for the small number of pupils with very low standards in reading, writing and mathematics. It was rare to find that their learning difficulties and needs had been carefully identified. These pupils need counselling to help them recognise their difficulties and believe that they are capable of learning.

Learning and teaching

36 Our Inspectors saw that teaching pupils in secure accommodation makes very high demands on teachers and those who help them. They have to work very hard and show a great deal of initiative and imagination to motivate pupils to take part in school activities. Each pupil has different educational needs, different educational experiences and qualifications and will be in the class for a different length of time. The best approach is where teachers and care staff work together to provide formal and informal education throughout the pupil's stay. For example, a great deal of social education can take place outside classrooms, especially in the evenings and at weekends.

37 The high quality teaching our Inspectors observed was directly related to the pupils high expectations (set by teachers) and to thorough, imaginative approaches to planning courses and lessons. Teachers make teaching work. Our Inspectors observed that the best teachers:

- are confident that the course is relevant for the group and for each pupil;
- divide the curriculum in several ways so that each member of the group can take part at their own level;
- convince pupils that they are committed to them;
- change the pace of each lesson;
- allow pupils to apply their learning, investigate, observe, experiment and draw conclusions;
- choose suitable resources to support learning and teaching;
- give real choice and encourage independent learning;
- maintain good standards of behaviour; and
- always praise pupils when they achieve something.

These approaches characterise good teaching in any situation and are particularly relevant where, as in secure accommodation, pupils have many special educational needs.

Accommodation

38 The shortage of suitable space for teaching is a major problem in each of the three main units. Some progress has been made in recent years to improve classroom facilities so that there is now a minimum standard of classrooms for general use and areas for home economics, science, technical education and physical education. However, providing for such a wide range of primary and secondary education needs makes considerable demands on space and facilities as well as on staff. The problems are made worse by the need for security and the need to have enough space and flexibility to deal with difficult behaviour. The cramped learning space in Rossie creates particular difficulties and priority should be given to replacing this with classrooms with enough room and storage space.

Staffing

39 Levels of staffing for education generally take account of:

- the emotional, behavioural and educational needs of pupils;
- how long they will be in secure care; and
- how long each teacher spends with each class.

Staffing levels must be high enough to make sure there are enough to:

- do the many duties associated with managing the curriculum;
- meet and report on the educational needs of pupils; and
- liaise with care and social work colleagues.

Staff must also find time to develop their skills.

40   To provide a reasonably broad curriculum, the schools need staff with a range of qualifications. In many cases, qualified primary teachers take extra training or gain experience in working with older pupils with learning difficulties. If those teachers are experienced and well supported, they have the advantage of being able to teach many subjects to their older pupils. However, specialists are needed to teach secondary courses which challenge and extend pupils. If they cannot take on a full-time member of staff in a particular subject, some units employ part-time tutors or arrange for local secondary schools to provide support. These arrangements should be considered more widely.

41   The units need a balance of teaching skills in English language, mathematics, science, technical education, home economics, computing and information technology, the arts and physical education. Most units have a core of experienced staff, but staff turnover has increased in recent years and this has affected the curriculum and morale. Inspectors found that there were shortages in science, social subjects, computing, music, modern foreign languages and religious and moral education.

Management and education
42   Recent inspections showed the important role played by heads of education. They are responsible for making sure that standards are high enough in the curriculum, in staff support and development and in planning for each pupil. In most secure units, there was no permanent management structure and the effects of this were seen across the school. In other units, the long-term benefits of effective management were obvious.

43   Heads of secure units did not pay enough attention to managing and assessing the curriculum. Curriculum policies did not give staff enough guidance on their work. And the systems for assessing pupils' progress and the effectiveness of the curriculum were weak. In one secure unit, as a result of encouragement and well-planned staff development, several teachers had made a huge contribution to improving the quality of the curriculum. Because of the demands on teachers, they must be supported by an active programme of staff development involving outside agencies. Secure unit staff can become isolated if they do not meet other teachers and receive advice and ideas from outside experts.

44   Senior management has an important role to play in encouraging co-operation between education and care staff. The key-worker scheme provides high levels of support to pupils, especially when care staff and teachers work closely together. Co-operation between care and educational staff tends to increase when they take part in joint projects which they can each contribute to and which produce good results. Our Inspectors found examples of successful joint approaches to assessment and personal and social development which demonstrated how successful this co-operation can be.

Recommendation 7

Greater priority should be given to improving education facilities in secure units. A new education block should be provided at Rossie as soon as possible.

Recommendation 8

More attention should be given to guiding the work of teachers and assuring quality in the curriculum. Teachers in secure units should have more opportunities for learning about developments in the national curriculum.

Recommendation 9

Education staff should be fully involved in designing assessment forms and procedures. All assessments and work with young people in secure care should be planned and carried out as a single approach to education, care and treatment. All staff should be aware of the main goals for each child and their role in helping the child to reach these goals.

Health

'Young people's health needs should be carefully identified and met; they should be encouraged to avoid health risks and to develop a healthy life-style.'

45   Young people in secure units have many of the health problems associated with their age group. But they are also more likely to have special health problems caused by bad experiences and moving from one care home to another. Many young people in secure care have experienced neglect, particularly when they were very young. And this neglect has often led to accidents and the child going into hospital. These problems have often been made worse by the child moving regularly from one care home to another, which means that they have not received regular and proper healthcare and advice.

Examinations and consultations

46   Young people normally have a routine medical examination within a week of going into secure care. This is usually carried out by the doctor in the secure unit or at the local health centre. However, arrangements for full medical examinations are less clear.

47   Our survey revealed that 90% of the young people had been medically examined during their current placement in secure accommodation. But 18% (13) of those did not have a 'freedom from infection' medical when they first arrived there. 15% (11) of the young people who had been examined had had a full medical examination (a detailed medical report including a medical history, the young person's general health, any medical care or treatment needed and, if necessary, an assessment to identify the need for medical action to help physical development, for example, to correct an eye squint). A further 8% (6) of the young people had been examined for specific health problems. Girls were more likely than boys to have a medical assessment when they arrived. But boys were more likely to have a full medical examination.

48   Of those young people who had been medically examined, 71% (52) received a 'clean bill of health'. Twenty-one young people had an illness or a special health need. The most common illnesses were asthma (5 out of 21) and skin complaints such as eczema. Seven of

the 21 had special health needs, including 4 cases of substance abuse. This figure is much lower than the 50% (45) of young people identified by heads of units as having problems with substance abuse.

49 'Another Kind of Home' included a recommendation that young people in residential care should be able to consult a doctor without having to explain why. Young people in secure care are normally registered with a local doctor. At the moment, they contact the GP through the key worker, unit manager or school nurse. They have to tell care staff why they want to see the doctor, and the staff then decide whether to contact the doctor. Different arrangements could be made so that the young person phones the doctor who then makes a decision about what action to take based on what the young person has said. In making arrangements for medical examinations, all the units take some account of the views of young people, particularly in relation to seeing a male or female doctor and where the examination should take place.

50 Where possible, the young people go to local dentists and opticians. However, dentists may not be willing to register young people because of changes in the NHS payment system. In this case, the young people are treated by the visiting community health dentist.

51 The healthcare needs of young people in secure care are now met in a similar way to those of other young people. However, more care needs to be taken to identify and make up for the neglect of health and dental needs in most of the young people's earlier lives.

Drug, alcohol and substance abuse
52 Heads of units said that half of the young people in secure accommodation were having problems with drug, alcohol or substance abuse. They also reported that these problems are usually known to the units either before the child arrives or within 24 hours. In almost all cases, the units considered that the information they received about the child's problem was enough for them to assess the child's needs and tackle them. But only one unit had a written policy on how to manage the problems associated with alcohol, drug and substance abuse. Further progress may have been made since the inspections.

53 Only one larger unit and two local units reported that their staff were trained to identify and cope with the unpredictable or disruptive behaviour which results from being drunk or using drugs or solvents. We have set up a national training programme for all residential child care staff. Heads of secure units should make sure that their staff, including education staff, are included in this programme.

54 To successfully introduce policies on drug, alcohol and substance abuse, there must be several courses of action including education programmes and one-to-one counselling. Above all, staff must support the policies actively because they have an important influence on the attitudes of the young people. Young people's knowledge and experience of drugs are also increasing. 'It is recognised that children from socially disadvantaged and dysfunctional families are far more likely to come into contact with the drug culture, to be drawn into drug misuse and experience its harmful consequences' (Drugs Task Force Report 1995, paragraph 3.4; see also paragraphs 3.29-3.31). Children in care find alcohol and other dangerous substances particularly attractive and are at risk of harming themselves

and others, including the risk of death. In the last three years, two young people in secure care have died as a direct result of drug, alcohol or substance abuse; one of them was on home leave.

55   Each unit should have a plan of action for dealing with drug, alcohol and substance abuse. This plan should cover both discouraging and preventing the abuse and coping with it, and it should be reviewed regularly. It should be part of the unit's general policies and involve joint action with local health, education and specialist agencies. It should concentrate particularly on how to assess and manage the risk which the young people may be to themselves and others while they are in the unit and when they leave. If this approach is to meet the needs of all the children in the unit, staff must have the necessary knowledge and skills and the confidence to use them. Each unit's staff training programme should include a focus on drug and alcohol abuse.

56   Our Inspectors considered that all the units could do the following.

- Ensure that placing authorities and unit managers tell those responsible for assessing social and healthcare needs about drug, alcohol and substance abuse problems in the young people who have just arrived.

- Make sure that those responsible for carrying out assessments and planning care have enough information about any drug, alcohol and substance abuse problems when the young person arrives in secure care.

- Extend and improve the knowledge and skills of those involved in assessment, planning care and introducing programmes, so that the services provided meet the needs of young people with drug, alcohol and substance abuse problems.

- Make better use of medical and other local specialist services.

Smoking

57   Many young people who go into secure care have been regular smokers for years. One unit has set a minimum age for smoking and has restricted smoking to one area. Another unit has followed the recommendation that staff should not smoke in the school. In another unit, all young people (with their parents' permission) and staff are allowed to smoke in common areas. Smoking policies should protect young people from the effects of passive smoking and should try to help smokers break the habit. The recommendations in 'Another Kind of Home' were designed to achieve this and should be introduced in secure units as in other homes and schools.

Records

58   Each unit holds medical files on the young people staying there. These files record medical examinations, recommended treatment and medication. They are usually kept by the school nurse or another member of staff. This arrangement means that the young person's records are confidential, but there are also disadvantages. Our Inspectors found that unless alternative arrangements have been made, it is very difficult for other members of staff to get at the records, for example to give out medication, if the person responsible for the records is off duty.

Recommendation 10

All care and education staff in secure units should receive training in how to deal with drug, alcohol and substance abuse.

Recommendation 11

Each unit's quality development plan should include a section on drug, alcohol and substance abuse which sets out targets for action and a timetable.

Mental health

59   Mental health problems drew the special attention of our Inspectors. Not enough is known about these problems in the secure units. Several of the people we talked to, including directors of social work and heads of units, questioned whether these problems should be tackled in secure units. This question was also raised by the Child Psychiatry Section of the Scottish Division of the Royal College of Psychiatrists. They suggested that we need to find out whether there are young people in secure accommodation with psychiatric problems whose needs might be better met somewhere else, for example by setting up an NHS secure unit in Scotland.

60   Psychological and psychiatric services are available to all secure units. These services have long-standing commitments to support staff and young people in all the main units.

They are used in a number of different ways, including:

- working directly with young people;
- acting as a consultant to key workers;
- preparing reports (mainly for Section 205 and 206 cases);
- going to review meetings;
- training and staff development;
- staff training; and
- staff counselling.

61   The records provided by consultant psychiatrists and psychologists for case files varied from reports required by us in Section 206 cases to occasional notes on other files. This lack of shared information cannot help the processes of assessment and planning. In addition there was little evidence of psychiatrists and psychologists working with other members of staff and agencies. As a result, the chance to improve ways of working with young people is being lost.

62   In one unit, the consultants claimed that their services were not used enough, particularly for assessing the young people when they arrived. They decided this was because there was no formal procedure for consulting them. There was evidence of units using some outside specialists, for example for drug counselling and sexual abuse counselling.

41

63   The Inspectors concluded that more could and should be done to involve psychologists and psychiatrists in the three larger units in particular.

Recommendation 12:

There should be further research into the mental health needs of children in secure accommodation and how these needs should be met.

Partnerships with parents

'Young people in secure care should be cared for in ways which maximise opportunities for parents continued involvement, and for care to be provided in the context of a partnership with parents wherever this is in the interests of the young person.'

64   The principle of working in partnership with parents is part of every unit's statement of aims and is described in information leaflets and brochures for parents. Parents are encouraged to visit and to keep in touch by phone. In general, they are automatically invited to review meetings on their child and are supported and encouraged to play an active part in all the important decisions.

65   Many units are trying to reduce parents' travel problems by arranging transport to and from the bus or railway station and by providing overnight accommodation. Visitors are welcome any day of the week between 9.30 am and 9.00 pm. The units do their very best to make parents feel comfortable and welcome. They can make special arrangements for family and friends who need help getting into or around the building because of a disability.

66   Parents and families are encouraged to get involved with their child during visits and can play table-tennis or pool, or share a meal. Birthdays and other family celebrations are important, so families are encouraged to visit on these occasions and are given every facility available to make it a happy time.

67   Key workers are encouraged to build and maintain links with young people's parents and families. If parents visit regularly, the young person and their key worker will also visit them at home. As the young person makes progress, parents and families are encouraged to take them walking in the school grounds or further away. This helps parents and families to share in the responsibility for the young person's care and control. Parents who do not contact the young person regularly will be visited by the key worker or local authority social worker and are encouraged to visit.

68   The young person's friends are only allowed to visit if they have been approved by the young person's parents and are introduced to the staff by the parents. If the unit decides to stop someone visiting the young person, or to restrict their visits, they explain this to the young person and the family and friends affected.

69   During their inspections, our Inspectors asked the views of some parents on the level of help and support they received from the care staff. The following comments sum up the generally positive response.

'If I have a problem, I can always get in touch and the care worker will come down to help and advise.'

'My son's development with the staff help has been excellent.'

'Everybody is helpful and everything is explained to you.'

Child centred collaboration

'Young people should be able to rely on a high quality of inter-disciplinary teamwork amongst the adults providing for their care, education and health needs.'

Co-operation with social workers

70   Replies to the questionnaires showed that the three larger units had had some problems working with social work staff. There were difficulties if the young person was not given a social worker, if the social worker did not keep in regular contact and if the social worker did not actively contribute to the care plan. The smaller units managed by the social work departments reported no such difficulties.

71   The inspection report on one of the larger units identified three problems which contributed to the breakdown of successful co-operation.

- Some young people blamed the social worker for their being in secure care.

- Care staff did not always welcome social workers when they visited.

- Some social workers did not seem sure of their role so stayed away.

72   Those problems need to be tackled.

- Before the young person goes into secure care, the social worker should explain the reasons for this. They key worker should explain again, repeating the same reasons, when the young person arrives in secure care.

- Care staff should be made fully aware of the need to co-operate with social workers.

- The role of social workers responsible for young people before, during and after secure care should be set out in local guidance.

We discuss the need for social workers to be more involved in chapter 3.

Co-operation between care and education staff

73   In recent years there has been a trend for care staff and teachers to work more closely together. They need to do more to share and understand each other's contribution to the young person's education and development. Our Inspectors found that teaching and care staff do not come together often enough to investigate areas of education which concerned both groups. The young people often take courses in personal and social development in classes and also in living units. But these courses were not drawn together in any way. The result is that some subjects such as drugs education and personal care are repeated, while there are gaps in other subjects such as diet, health and sexuality.

A feeling of safety

'Young people and children should feel safe in any residential home or school.'

74   Young people who go into secure care may well feel safer than they have for a long time. They are partly protected from the pressures of the outside world and many experience a sense of relief that their own behaviour is no longer out of control. That feeling should be maintained and the young people protected from any threats of bullying by other young people or by staff. There must be a balance between the demands of security and the need to create, as far as possible, the atmosphere of a residential home for children.

75   The security arrangements in secure accommodation are based on government guidance. This guidance sets standards for doors, windows, alarms, security outside the building and so on. The units have reacted quickly in the past to recommendations for improving security. But they could not be considered escape proof. From time to time, young people have been known to break through the security and run away from the unit. There have been very few cases where young people have attacked members of staff to try and steal keys and break out of the building.

76   More often children try to escape while they are at home on leave or are on outings supervised by staff. Whenever a young person escapes, the unit examines the decisions it has made in the case and in allowing the young person out of the unit. This will generally lead to changes in the arrangements for the young person so that they do not escape again.

77   Containing and controlling very difficult behaviour is a daily issue for secure units. We are contributing our full share to a £500,000 UK training package on this subject which will be made widely available to residential units in 1996 to 97. Guidance on setting limits to behaviour in residential child care will be provided in 1996 by the Scottish Office. Secure units have skill and experience in this area and must make sure that their methods are up to date and effective. Each unit should review its approach twice a year.

78   Rossie school has an isolation cell to control very difficult behaviour for short periods. The conditions in this cell are not right for children and its use and design should be reviewed and changed.

Recommendation 13

The use and design of the isolation cell at Rossie should be reviewed and changed.

79   Whether young people feel safe and the unit is secure depends on the number of staff available as well as the quality of their work. The 1985 Code of Practice said that as a minimum there should be at least two members of staff to any one group of children during working hours. How many young people there should be in the group was not made clear. There has been no more specific guidance since 1985. The heads of the three larger secure units believe that there should be at least three care staff to eight young people. And there should be a team leader responsible for a shift of 9 staff and 24 young people. In practice staffing levels often fall below this standard.

80   As the Inspectors noted in one unit:

> 'On paper the staff to child ratio of 1:2 is consistent with the nature of care and security that has to be provided. However, the realities of staff leave, sickness, in-service training, and key worker commitments outwith the units reduce it at times to 1:4. This must be considered dangerously thin and puts too heavy and inappropriate a reliance on the young people to conform. Such staff levels also make it impossible for any counselling work with individual young people to be undertaken.'

Recommendation 14

Managers of secure units and local authorities should make sure that the unit can meet the minimum requirement of two staff to any one group of children during waking hours. In doing so, they must allow for sickness, leave and training. Normally they should plan for three care staff to eight young people. The exact arrangements should depend on the care and education system in the unit.

Chapter 3

Key points for a plan of action

General

1   We concluded, at the end of Chapter 1, that the priorities were:

- to improve the availability of secure care places when they are needed;

- to deal earlier and more effectively with criminal behaviour;

- to improve assessment and planning for young people who need compulsory care; and

- to develop the role of residential schools for young people with disturbed behaviour who commit crimes.

In this chapter we recommend key points for a plan of action to meet these goals.

Improving the availability of places

2   We recommend three approaches to improving availability.

- Increasing investment in maintaining existing units so that beds are not out of use for long periods. This could increase availability by up to 5%.

- Developing community-based projects as an alternative to secure care whenever suitable. These projects need to be carefully targeted if they are to make a real impact on the use of secure care. Their true effect is difficult to assess. If there were well-targeted projects they could reduce the demand by 5%.

- Improving training and service planning for secure unit staff so that they can deal with the most challenging behaviour and their work is focused on what is needed to change that behaviour. In this way, the child will be able to move on to other forms of care and education more quickly. This should reduce the length of time a child stays in secure care by about 10% and so should increase availability by about 10%.

3   Taken together, these three approaches could improve availability by 20%, which is the equivalent of 18 extra places. Each approach is described in more detail below with specific recommendations. We also recommend new arrangements for monitoring free places and the numbers of young people going into secure care.

Making as many of the existing places available as possible

4   The first priority is to make sure that all secure care beds which are free are available for use and to reduce the times when beds are out of use. In 1994 to 95 six secure care beds were out of use for several weeks because the unit needed repairs or improvements. Six beds out of a total of 89 is quite a loss and emphasises the need to set aside enough money for repairs and improvements.

5   The Scottish Office is responsible for all major spending on buildings and equipment for secure units. Between 1990 and 1994 the total spent was £1.9 million on all four units, including £1.4 million for building St Katherine's in Edinburgh which added five places. There was also about £130,000 for improvements, maintenance and repairs for the three main units. Given their task, the units are bound to have high maintenance and repair costs, and the work has to be done quickly so that the buildings are always secure. The children's environment should build up their respect for themselves and others. The three large units each have serious problems in providing such an environment.

6   Repairs and maintenance decisions should be made quickly and on the spot. Officers in charge should have a large enough budget to allow them to meet this responsibility and make minor changes and improvements. Units should not have to apply to the Scottish Office for permission for projects under £150,000.

Extending existing units

7   Building new secure accommodation is expensive. A feasibility study for replacing St Mary's, Kenmure has been carried out and the recommendation for this set out the main requirements for any new secure accommodation:

> 'The aim should be to create as normal a living environment as possible wherein necessary security and safety measures are as unobtrusive as possible. Both internally and externally the building should appear aesthetically pleasing.
>
> The design must create an atmosphere and an environment which allows young people to maximise the positive input obtained from a period in care. Young people, their families and staff require adequate living and recreation space allowing personal privacy for residents, adequate educational and training facilities to allow residents to maximise their potential, adequate visiting facilities to allow family relationships to be maintained, adequate work space for staff to relate to young people both as individuals and in groups. High walls and fences should be avoided.
>
> The design must take account of the need to provide the highest possible standard of security both internally and externally. Internally ceiling heights, window designs, locking systems, and general lay out must emphasise the need for security. Externally, roof designs must be such that they cannot be climbed either by residents or by non-residents from outwith the building. Externally, windows and doors must be tamper proof and all round visibility externally by cameras, is essential for staff on duty internally.'

The cost of providing a new secure unit to meet this brief and Department of Health standards is about £250,000 for each bed.

8   Increasing the number of places provided in existing units is a more realistic goal. But it is still costly. Also, St Mary's, Kenmure and Kerelaw have problems with their present design as we highlighted in chapter 2. Both are more like small prisons than secure accommodation for children and have major problems in providing an environment in which young people will build respect for others and themselves. In view of their design faults and their practical problems, we consider that they need to be replaced. This may not be possible immediately, but it will be necessary at some point, so plans for any extra secure

care places should be co-ordinated with plans to replace the units. From the feasibility study for replacing St Mary's, Kenmure with a new 30-bed unit (providing another six places), we estimate that the cost is likely to be about £7.5 million.

9   In some ways Rossie School causes less serious problems. However, it too falls well short of current design standards and there is not enough separate space for girls. The education facilities are completely unsuitable and there is no scope for improving them without providing a new education unit. This could be done in a straightforward way by building on the ground where the old open school was demolished. This should be given priority so that Rossie can deal with the educational needs of its young people. There should be a feasibility study for building new educational facilities at Rossie.

10   Some people have argued that the three main units should be replaced with smaller local units. They point to the success of the Edinburgh units as a model of how to develop resources in the future. Small units do have an important role and there would be value in more developments similar to the Edinburgh units and the associated close support units. However, they can only handle some needs, they operate on a short-term basis and they cannot meet the standards required at a realistic cost. Larger units are the most practical option, but they need smaller social care units within them to meet the needs of young people sensitively and effectively.

11   To keep the current number of places at the correct standards with a small increase in numbers and an increase in availability will require a major building programme. This would have to be funded through a combination of public and private finance. This will lead to increases in the rates which the units charge. But we estimate that the increased total weekly cost would still be lower than the average cost of secure care in England.

Recommendation 15

Priority should be given to increasing repair, maintenance and furnishing budgets in existing units. In this way, we can reduce the time when beds are out of use.

Recommendation 16

The priorities in a redevelopment plan should be:

- **a new education block at Rossie;**

- **replacing St Mary's, Kenmure on the existing site; and**

- **replacing Kerelaw on a site closer to the areas from which most of the young people come.**

Developing community-based care

12   Article 40 of the UN Convention on the Rights of the Child says that:

'A variety of dispositions, such as care, guidance and supervision orders; counselling; probation; foster care; education and vocational training programmes and other alternatives to institutional care shall be available to ensure that children are dealt with in a manner appropriate to their well-being and proportionate both to their circumstances and the offence.'

13   The alternative care available for young people should be widened and developed so that secure care is only used as a last resort and for the shortest possible time. Demand must be managed better to make the most of the limited and expensive number of places available. The support of community-based care is important here, as is developing the role of residential schools.

14   There are encouraging examples of new models of child care that are dealing with children who could have gone into secure care. And there are also several foster carers who have been recruited to work with particularly difficult young people as an alternative to secure care. Two developments are particularly impressive.

Intensive support units

15   Intensive support units are children's homes with a large staff. They are designed to look after four to six young people and work closely with a secure unit. These intensive support units have a number of possible roles, including:

- caring for young people with serious behaviour problems who could end up in secure care;

- an alternative to secure care, for instance when the interests of a young person under a secure care order could be better met in open accommodation; or

- an after-care service for young people coming out of secure accommodation.

Intensive day programmes

16   The Scottish Office is funding two intensive community-based day programmes. The first of these is a project in the West of Scotland working with 16- and 17-year-old offenders. The second is a joint project between the police and social workers to work with regular offenders in Central Region. There are other examples of community-based projects dealing with the needs and problems of young people whose behaviour could lead them into secure care. But we are still a long way from having the alternatives available in most local authority areas.

Recommendation 17

Close support units should be developed in each Scottish city to meet the need for intensive care and control of some young people over short periods.

Recommendation 18

Local authorities and others should continue to develop community-based care projects for young people who would otherwise end up in secure accommodation. The results of these projects must be assessed.

Monitoring free places and the number of young people going into secure care
17   Whilst carrying out this review, we found it difficult to gather together all the relevant information about the use of secure accommodation for children. We were also aware that there was no summary of units with a high demand or free places at any given time. There would be advantages in having a single contact point for information about all young

people going into secure care across Scotland so that best use could be made of all available resources. This would also mean that patterns of demand could be monitored and secure care could be managed better. This could be done by setting up a Secure Accommodation Admissions Bureau, probably in one of the large units, with phone and possibly other links to all the units and local authorities. The Bureau would be responsible for keeping an up-to-date record of free places and places being taken up and would serve as the first point of contact for any agency wanting to send a child to secure care. In the secure units run by local authorities the chief social work officers would usually arrange for young people to enter a unit before contacting the Bureau, but they would need to let the Bureau know as soon as possible. The Bureau would not be involved in assessment or giving advice.

Recommendation 19

The Scottish Office, should, in consultation with local authorities and the secure units, set up a Secure Accommodation Admissions Bureau to serve as the first point of contact for any agency wanting to send a child to secure care. The Bureau should also monitor demand and produce monthly reports.

Improving care and education in secure units
Staffing and training
18   Staffing is the main cost of providing secure care. Local authorities cover most of the costs of keeping a child in secure accommodation and they negotiate rates with each unit. Our Inspectors noted that staffing levels often fell below the standard of having three care staff to every eight young people.

19   In 1993 to 94 the Government introduced a grant for training in residential child care. This has mostly been used for training local authority staff. But it should also be used to cover the training costs for services provided by voluntary and private organisations. Local authorities are encouraged to recognise the costs of training needs when negotiating their contracts with the units. Some progress has been made in improving the training of residential child-care staff, but there is still much to be done. Local authorities should treat secure accommodation staff as a priority group, even if the staff are not employed by the local authority. Local authorities must make clear in their contracts with voluntary organisations how much of the payment will go towards staff training and what kind of training this will be. Progress should then be monitored. All units should include training targets in their quality development plans.

20   The training targets for the Government grant relate to training for child care and social work in many different settings. Training for the special work involved in secure care must also be improved. As part of this aim, funding should be made available to develop training programmes specifically for staff working in secure care.

Recommendation 20

Special training options for staff in secure care units should be developed.

Quality development plan

21   Each secure unit has a statement of functions and aims. By using this base and consulting local authorities, each secure unit should draw up a quality development plan. These plans should identify the recommendations of all inspections and should set out a clear plan of action for each one. The quality development plan should also list other key priorities for improving the performance of the unit. These priorities should be based on the unit's own analysis of its strengths and weaknesses.

22   Quality development plans should improve the quality of the care provided. We have also noted that there is a need to 'enhance the capability of children's secure care units to contain and treat particularly challenging and difficult young people'. This means that each of the three large units should review its statement of functions and aims and its strengths and weaknesses. They should then look at what steps can and should be taken to improve their performance. In particular they should look at the mix of professional skills they need to carry out their roles properly, taking into account the need for a range of skills other than social work and teaching. Managers of the units should consult local authorities and other agencies before finalising their statement of functions and aims. They should then send their statements to the new National Planning Group (see below). Once they have the Planning Group's agreement, the units should include the changes in their quality development plans.

Inspections and supervision

23   Under the regulations, all secure accommodation must be approved by the Secretary of State. We inspect each unit every three years. Local authority care homes which include secure units are also inspected twice a year by the local authority's own inspection unit. Since 1992 all children's homes in Scotland, except the independent secure units, have been inspected twice a year. The two independent units, Rossie and St Mary's, Kenmure, are only inspected every three years.

24   It is not right that the independent secure units should be inspected less often than other forms of residential care for children. This arrangement should be changed in the review of inspection due in 1997. The three-yearly inspections by us and HM Inspectors of Schools should continue.

Recommendation 21

Staff training in secure units should be improved by:
- managers of secure units introducing plans to meet the national targets for training residential child care staff by 1999; and

- local authorities giving priority to training grants for staff in secure units, including units run by independent agencies.

Recommendation 22

Each secure unit should review its statement of functions and objectives and should decide what action it needs to take to be able to deal with the most challenging behaviour.

Recommendation 23

Each secure unit should draw up a quality-development plan for introducing a range of improvements. It should review its plan every three months.

Getting involved earlier and more effectively

25   In most cases young people who go into secure care already have a long history of problems, disturbed behaviour and criminal offences. It is important that children should not be labelled by their difficulties. But they must be assessed as early as possible and action must be taken to prevent their problems getting worse.

26   To achieve this effectively, staff may have to change their attitudes as well as their procedures. Social work and education agencies must develop new procedures which provide for better assessment at an earlier stage and for effective action before patterns of problem behaviour are established.

27   These issues were well recognised by Lord Kilbrandon 25 years ago when he wrote his report which set up the Children's Hearings system. At the end of the report, Kilbrandon says:

> 'Society is, we believe, seriously concerned to secure a more effective and discriminating machinery for intervention for the avoidance and reduction of juvenile delinquency .....
>
> From the earliest age of understanding, every child finds himself part of a given family and a given environment – factors which are beyond his or society's power to control. During childhood the child is subject to the influences of home and school. Where these have for whatever reason fallen short or failed, the precise means by which the special needs of this minority of children are brought to light are equally largely fortuitous. The individual need may at that stage differ in degree, but scarcely in essential character, and such children may be said at present to be, more than most, in a real and special sense 'hostages to fortune'. The time has come, we believe, when society may reasonably be expected so to organise its affairs as to reduce the arbitrary effects of what is still too often a haphazard detection process; and consequently to extend to this minority of children, within a sustained and continuing discipline of social education, the measures which their needs dictate, and of which they have hitherto been too often deprived.'

28   These words are highly relevant. Much of Kilbrandon's vision is not yet reality. Kilbrandon expected that there would be very close co-operation between social work and education from the early years. This co-operation has not always happened, but it is an important part of taking effective action early in a child's life. Many authorities have good links between social work and education for older children, but few have effective arrangements for younger children. More detailed work is needed in this area and we consider this should be given the highest priority.

Recommendation 24

Local authorities should review their arrangements for co-operation between social work and education departments in assessing and treating primary school children with serious behavioural difficulties. They should complete these reviews by December 1996 and report the outcomes to The Scottish Office by February 1997.

Recommendation 25

We should commission a review of the research on providing early help for children with serious behavioural problems. After the local authority reviews have been done, we should hold a national seminar for social work and education authorities to decide on a plan of action.

Improving assessment and care plans

29   We need to improve assessment and care planning if we are to deal successfully with the complex problems of the young people. Assessment is one of the most important social work tasks. It provides a basis for planning and decision-making in a number of settings. Social work agencies collect detailed information for assessment, but they do not always interpret this information or use it to develop detailed plans.

30   To properly assess and plan for a child in care, both residential care staff and social workers must be involved. If we want to free more secure places we must not allow children to stay in secure accommodation any longer than is necessary. Plans for each child need to be made and carried out quickly. We found that social workers and residential care staff did not communicate well or always have a successful working arrangement, probably because they did not see their duties in the same way and did not keep in touch with each other.

31   Secure units reported that social workers visited on average once a month, often for formal reviews and planning meetings but they spent little time working directly with the child. Social workers should take part in drawing up the detailed care plan with the secure unit and should visit often to work directly with the child and monitor the progress of the care plan with residential staff. For children in secure care, the social worker should visit at least once every two weeks, and once a week for the first six weeks. This is to make sure that effective care plans are made and carried out quickly. It is justified because the numbers are small and the cost of secure care is high. If social workers and residential care staff can work together more successfully, the child will receive better care and should be able to move on at the earliest possible stage.

Recommendation 26

Young people's care needs should be assessed and planned more effectively by:

- more training;
- adopting a common style for assessments in secure units;
- including social workers in the assessment and care plan; and
- social workers visiting children in secure units every week for the first six weeks and then at least once every two weeks.

Residential schools

32   Research shows that residential education is an effective form of care and can have successful results for troubled young people with problems which are difficult to manage. Sometimes, however, the authorities are not keen to consider early enough the value of

placing a child in residential care or a residential school. When we examined the five cases mentioned in Chapter 2 and the young people in secure units generally, it is clear that many of these young people might never have gone into secure care if there had been other residential placements available which could offer stable and consistent care and education and manage challenging behaviour.

33   Local and national education and social work agencies share responsibility for residential schools. Their policies and practices should be well co-ordinated. This is not always the case. Many authorities already have procedures for jointly assessing young people with a range of difficulties, and some have joint funding arrangements for residential care. Many of the new local authorities will be too small to provide a range of residential care for children. They will need to plan with other authorities and with voluntary care providers how to meet the different needs of the children from their area. Under the Children (Scotland) Act 1995, local authorities will have to prepare and publish plans for child care services. Secure accommodation for children should be seen as a part of the range of residential school care for children and not as a separate institution.

34   Between 1964 and 1984, the Social Work Services Group (SWSG) had most of the responsibility for the List D schools and secure units. Since 1984, its role has been restricted and its financial responsibilities for secure care have been transferred to local authorities. With increased demand and more local authorities, we now need a new system of co-ordination to make sure that the services in this area develop properly. We recommend setting up a National Planning Group with representatives from each of the relevant agencies – social work, education, police, Children's Hearings and the main units – to plan and develop care and education services for young people with behavioural problems which include offending. The Planning Group should pay particular attention to developing more effective, earlier intervention.

Recommendation 27

The new local authority children's services plans should recognise the value of residential schools for children with particularly difficult behaviour and should set out how the authority will pay for places for children who need them.

Recommendation 28

A National Planning Group should be set up to oversee the planning, management and development of secure units and care and education services for young people with behavioural problems which include offending. They should pay special attention to developing more effective, early intervention. The Planning Group should report each year to the Secretary of State.

List of recommendations

1   Each year, police and social work departments should review the arrangements and practice in each force area for children who need to be held in a place of safety before appearing in a court. They should make sure that policies and practice are well co-ordinated and plan and review any improvements which are needed.

2   Secure units should review their arrangements for co-ordinating assessments of young people.

3   The main secure units should, after consulting local authorities, develop and agree on standard admission forms and assessment procedures.

4   Local authorities should give units as much information as possible on each child before the child arrives in secure care. The authorities should complete this information within two working days.

5   Each child in secure accommodation should have their own programme of care, education and treatment which meets their needs and aims to change the behaviour which led to them being in secure care. The programme should be decided at the end of the assessment and every member of staff should be told the aims and how they can help.

6   Local authorities should consult secure units to agree standards for arranging aftercare and education for the children leaving secure care.

7   Greater priority should be given to improving education facilities in secure units. A new education block should be provided at Rossie as soon as possible.

8   More attention should be given to guiding the work of teachers and assuring quality in the curriculum. Teachers in secure units should have more opportunities for learning about developments in the national curriculum.

9   Education staff should be fully involved in designing assessment forms and procedures. All assessments and work with young people in secure care should be planned and carried out as a single approach to education, care and treatment. All staff should be aware of the main goals for each child and their role in helping the child to reach these goals.

10 All care and education staff in secure units should receive training in how to deal with drug, alcohol and substance abuse.

11 Each unit's quality development plan should include a section on drug, alcohol and substance abuse which sets out targets for action and a timetable.

12 There should be further research into the mental health needs of children in secure accommodation and how these needs should be met.

13 The use and design of the isolation cell at Rossie should be reviewed and changed.

14 Managers of secure units and local authorities should make sure that the unit can meet the minimum requirement of two staff to any one group of children during waking hours. In doing so, they must allow for sickness, leave and training. Normally they should plan for three care staff to eight young people. The exact arrangements should depend on the care and education system in the unit.

15 Priority should be given to increasing repair, maintenance and furnishing budgets in existing units. In this way, we can reduce the time when beds are out of use.

16 The priorities in a redevelopment plan should be:
   • a new education block at Rossie;
   • replacing Kenmure St Mary's on the existing site; and
   • replacing Kerelaw on a site closer to the areas from which most of the young people come.

17 Close support units should be developed in each Scottish city to meet the need for intensive care and control of some young people over short periods.

18 Local authorities and others should continue to develop community-based care projects for young people who would otherwise end up in secure accommodation. The results of these projects must be assessed.

19 The Scottish Office should, in consultation with local authorities and the secure units set up a Secure Accommodation Admissions Bureau to serve as the first point of contact for any agency wanting to send a child to secure care. The Bureau should also monitor demand and produce monthly reports.

20 Special training options for staff in secure care units should be developed.

21 Staff training in secure units should be improved by:
   • managers of secure units introducing plans to meet the national targets for training residential child care staff by 1999; and
   • local authorities giving priority to training grants for staff in secure units, including units run by independent agencies.

22 Each secure unit should review its statement of functions and aims and should decide what action it needs to take to be able to deal with the most challenging behaviour.

23 Each secure unit should draw up a quality-development plan for introducing a range of improvements. It should review its plan every three months.

24   Local authorities should review their arrangements for co-operation between social work and education departments in assessing and treating primary school children with serious behavioural difficulties. They should complete these reviews by December 1996 and report the results to The Scottish Office by February 1997.

25   The Scottish Office should commission a review of the research on early intervention with children with serious behavioural problems. After the local authority reviews are completed The Scottish Office should hold a national seminar for social work and education authorities to decide on a plan of action.

26   Young people's care needs should be assessed and planned more effectively by:

- more training;

- adopting a common style for assessments in secure units;

- including social workers in the assessment and care plan; and

- social workers visiting children in secure units every week for the first six weeks and then as a minimum fortnightly.

27   The new local authority children's services plans should recognise the value of residential schools for children with particularly difficult behaviour and should set out how the authority will pay for places for children who need them.

28   A National Planning Group should be set up to oversee the planning, management and development of secure units and care and education services for young people with behavioural problems which include offending. They should pay special attention to developing more effective, early intervention. The Planning Group should report each year to the Secretary of State.

Index of recommendations

Index of figures

A brief history of Rossie

(Taken from a poster at Rossie)

'Rossie opened in May 1857 and owes its existence to Colonel MacDonald of Rossie and St Martin's. It was set up to reform young offenders who, after being convicted of crime and passing through a term of imprisonment, were transferred from jail to spend a period of years at Rossie Reformatory. In 1860 new premises were opened creating accommodation for sixty-five boys. At this time the farm that was worked by the boys extended to forty acres.

In 1911, Jack Carson became Headmaster and soon replaced the cat-o-nine tails with the tawse and closed the stone quarry in which the boys laboured. He remained in this post well into the 1930s and by 1937 the reformatory was known as Rossie Farm School and had been reclassified as an Approved School. The Juvenile Courts now sent children to Rossie for training. 1939 saw a new building erected next to the old reformatory that was able to accommodate over one hundred boys and the farm now extended to five hundred acres.

In 1957 the School celebrated its centenary by opening another building – the Glenmarkie Wing. In those first one hundred years three thousand boys had passed through the doors of Rossie.

Shortly afterwards the first Secure Unit in the whole of the UK was established at Rossie. Following the 1968 Social Work (Scotland) Act, Rossie became known as a List 'D' School. Further development in 1975 allowed an increase of ten places in the secure unit.

Rossie continued as a List 'D' School until 1984/85 when the main part of the School closed. In 1986 Rossie started to admit girls. Today Rossie remains one of the three larger Secure Units in Scotland and presently caters for thirty young people; twenty-five in security within the Old MacDonald Wing and five in Forth House, the open unit. The estate managed by the School is presently one hundred acres.'

UN Convention on the Rights of the Child

Article 37: Torture and deprivation of liberty

States Parties shall ensure that:

    (a) no child shall be subjected to torture or other cruel, inhuman or degrading treatment or punishment. Neither capital punishment nor life imprisonment without possibility of release shall be imposed for offences committed by persons below 18 years of age.

    (b) no child shall be deprived of his or her liberty unlawfully or arbitrarily. The arrest, detention or imprisonment of a child shall be in conformity with the law and shall be used only as a measure of last resort and for the shortest appropriate period of time.

    (c) every child deprived of liberty shall be treated with humanity and respect for the inherent dignity of the human person, and in a manner which takes into account the needs of persons of their age. In particular every child deprived of liberty shall be separated from adults unless it is considered in the child's best interest not to do so and shall have the right to maintain contact with his or her family through correspondence and visits, save in exceptional circumstances.

    (d) every child deprived of his or her liberty shall have the right to prompt access to legal and other appropriate assistance as well as the right to challenge the legality of the deprivation of his or her liberty before a court or other competent, independent and impartial authority and to a prompt decision on any such action.

Article 40: Administration of juvenile justice

1. States Parties recognise the right of every child alleged as, accused of, or recognised as having infringed the penal law, to be treated in a manner consistent with the promotion of the child's sense of dignity and worth, which reinforces the child's respect for the human rights and fundamental freedoms of others and which takes into account the child's age and the desirability of promoting the child's re-integration and the child's assuming a constructive role in society.

2. (Mainly concerns proceedings with regard to evidence and court proceedings.)

3. States Parties shall seek to promote the establishment of laws, procedures, authorities and institutions specifically applicable to children alleged as, accused of, or recognised as having infringed the penal law, and in particular:

    (a) the establishment of a minimum age below which children shall be presumed not to have the capacity to infringe the penal law;

(b) whenever appropriate and desirable, measures for dealing with such children without resorting to judicial proceedings, providing that human rights and legal safeguards are fully respected.

4. A variety of dispositions, such as care, guidance and supervision orders; counselling; probation; foster care; education and vocational training programmes and other alternatives to institutional care shall be available to ensure that children are dealt with in a manner appropriate to their well-being and proportionate both to their circumstances and the offence.

Social Work (Scotland) Act 1968: Section 58

Residence in Secure Accommodation

58A (1) A child who is made subject to a supervision requirement under this Act may not be placed or kept in secure accommodation, except under the provisions of this Act.

(2) In this Act, "secure accommodation" means accommodation provided in a residential establishment in accordance with regulations made under section 60(1) of this Act for the purpose of restricting the liberty of children.

(3) Where a children's hearing decide, in accordance with section 44 of this Act, that a child is in need of compulsory measures of care, and they are satisfied that either -

    (a) he has a history of absconding, and

        (i) he is likely to abscond unless he is kept in secure accommodation; and

        (ii) if he absconds, it is likely that his physical, mental or moral welfare will be at risk; or

    (b) he is likely to injure himself or other persons unless he is kept in secure accommodation,

        they may make it a condition of a supervision requirement under subsection (1)(b) of the said section 44 that the child shall be liable to be placed and kept in secure accommodation in the named residential establishment at such times as the person in charge of that establishment, with the agreement of the director of social work of the local authority required to give effect to the supervision requirement, considers it necessary that he do so.

(4) The Secretary of State shall have power by regulations to make provision with respect to the placing in secure accommodation of any child -

    (a) who is subject to a supervision requirement imposed under section 44 of this Act but not subject to a condition imposed under subsection (3) of this section; or

    (b) who is not subject to such a supervision requirement but who is being cared for by a local authority or voluntary organisation in pursuance of such enactments as may be specified in the regulations.

and such regulations shall specify the circumstances which require to pertain before a child may be so placed under regulations made under this subsection and may specify different circumstances for different cases or classes of case.

Time limits on keeping without reference to children's hearing

58B – (1) The Secretary of State shall by regulations prescribe -

> (a) the maximum period during which a child may be kept under this Act in secure accommodation without the authority of a children's hearing or of the sheriff.

> (b) the period within which the case of a child placed under this Act in secure accommodation shall be referred to the reporter and different periods may be prescribed in respect of different cases or classes of case.

(2) The Secretary of State shall by regulations make provision to enable a child who has been placed in secure accommodation under section 58A(4) of this Act or his parent to require that the child's case be brought before a children's hearing within a shorter period than would otherwise apply under regulations made under subsection (1)(a) of this section.

(3) Where, in any case, a children's hearing directs the reporter to make application to the sheriff for a finding under section 42(2)(c) of this Act (finding that grounds for referral are established), they shall have power, if they are satisfied with regard to the criteria specified in paragraph (a) or (b) of section 58A(3) of this Act, to order that, pending the determination of his case in accordance with section 42(5) or (6) of this Act, the child shall be liable to be placed and kept in secure accommodation in a named residential establishment at such times as the person in charge of that establishment with the agreement of the director of social work of the local authority for the area of the children's hearing, considers necessary.

Review of secure accommodation condition

58C – (1) A condition imposed under section 58A(3) of this Act, requiring a child to reside in secure accommodation, shall be subject to review by a children's hearing at such time as the local authority recommends and otherwise at such times and in accordance with such provisions as the Secretary of State shall by regulations prescribe.

(2) A condition to which this section applies shall be reviewed when the supervision requirement is being reviewed, and may be reviewed separately from that review.

(3) A condition to which this section applies shall cease to have effect at the expiry of the period of three months after it was made, unless it has been reviewed and the condition has been ordered to continue.

(4) A condition which is continued on review shall cease to have effect at the expiry of the period of -

> (a) nine months after it is first reviewed;

> (b) 12 months after the second or any subsequent review,

unless it has been reviewed and the condition has been ordered to continue.

(5) Sections 44 and 48(5) of this Act shall apply to the review of conditions made under section 58A(3) of this Act as they apply to the review of supervision requirements.

(6) The Secretary of State may from time to time make regulations to vary the periods specified in this section.

Sheriff's power to direct to cease to have effect

58D. Where under section 49(5) of this Act (appeal against decision of children's hearing) the sheriff is satisfied in a case in which there is in force a condition under section 58A(3) of this Act that the decision of the children's hearing is not justified in all the circumstances of the case he shall direct that the condition shall cease to have effect.

Warrants to detain in secure accommodation

58E – (1) Where the sheriff or a children's hearing issues a warrant under any of section 37, 40 and 42 of this Act (detention in a place of safety), he or they may, if satisfied with regard to the criteria specified in paragraph (a) or (b) of section 58A(3) of this Act, order that the child shall be liable to be placed and kept in secure accommodation in a named residential establishment at such times as the person in charge of that establishment, with the agreement of the director of social work of the local authority, considers necessary. The local authority referred to in this subsection is, in the case of a warrant issued or renewed by the sheriff, the local authority for the area of the children's hearing which was dealing with the child in respect of whom the warrant was issued and, in the case of a warrant issued or renewed by a children's hearing, the local authority for the area of that children's hearing.

(2) For the purposes of this section, the Secretary of State may make regulations amending, varying or displaying any of the criteria specified in the said paragraphs (a) and (b) of section 58A(3) of this Act except in relation to a warrant under section 37 of this Act.

Procedures for placing in secure accommodation

58F – (1) The Secretary of State may by regulations make provision for the procedures to be applied in the placing of children in secure accommodation, and without prejudice to the foregoing generality may make provision for the referral of cases to a children's hearing for review.

(2) Regulations under this section may specify the duties of the reporter in relation to the placing of children in secure accommodation.

(3) Regulations under this section may make provision for the parent of a child being informed of the placing of the child in secure accommodation.

Transitional provisions

58G Regulations made under sections 58A to 58F of this Act may include such transitional provisions as the Secretary of State may consider necessary, including provisions varying the application of any provision in those sections for a transitional period, either generally, or in relation to specified classes of cases.

The number of young people going into secure care between 1990 and 1995

Table 1: by age (1 April 1990 to 31 March 1995)

Age	1990 to 91	1991 to 92	1992 to 93	1993 to 94	1994 to 95
0-11	2	3	2	8	10
12	10	3	3	13	11
13	16	17	11	34	28
14	55	36	40	70	50
15	96	93	72	132	107
16	66	85	55	30	15
17	5	5	12	4	0
18+	0	1	2	0	0
Not Known	0	0	0	0	2
Total	250	243	197	291	223

Table 2: by statute (1 April 1990 to 31 March 1995)

Statute	1990 to 91	1991 to 92	1992 to 93	1993 to 94	1994 to 95
Section 413	0	1	2	2	2
Section 205	0	2	0	0	0
Section 206	4	12	6	8	12
Section 44 (1) (b)	79	65	31	93	30
Place of Safety (Social Work Act)	45	49	33	64	57
Place of Safety (Criminal Justice Act)	50	9	30	34	68
Authority of Director	62	60	79	72	34
Other	10	45	16	18	20
Total	250	243	197	291	223

Association of Directors of Social Work Survey of secure care April 1995

Strathclyde, Shetland, Orkney, Fife, Tayside, Grampian, Lothian and Borders returned their answers to the survey.

Children in secure accommodation on 10 April 1995.

	Boys	Girls
Hearings route		
Section 58E	5	2
Section 58A	36	20
Court route		
Section 206		
Section 205		
Section 24	9	2
Section 297	2	
Section 413	3	
Bail condition	2	
Total	59	24

At the time of the survey some beds were out of use, so the answers received show that the units were full. Sixty-three young people were in secure care as a result of orders made by the hearings and 20 as a result of orders made by the court. Seven of the hearings were 58 Es (emergency placements) and four of the court placements were remands (S24 and S297).

Another 24 children (including 6 girls) had a condition allowing secure care attached to their supervision order. But they had not been put in to secure care. Of these children:

- six had been placed in an open school on trial following a period in secure care;

- ten had been placed in open schools or resource centres with extra support because secure care was not seen as being in their best interests;

- four were placed in residential schools or resource centres because no secure place was available;

- one was sent home because no secure place was available; and

- one was placed in Longriggend because no secure place was available.

In two cases (from Grampian) it was not known where the young people had been placed.

The survey also estimated that Children's Hearings had made 154 secure care authorisations between April 1994 and April 1995. Forty of these were girls and 114 were boys.

Designed & Produced on behalf of The Scottish Office by HMSO Scotland, J3987, 6/96 (122665)